HEALING AND PROPHECY AT MEHU:

The Life and Work of Prophet Jenasman Kwadwo Amoaforo

Kathleen O'Brien Wicker
Kofi Asare Opoku
Margaret Naiandrina Streetor

Sub-Saharan Publishers – Accra Ghana

First published in Ghana in 2012 by
Sub-Saharan Publishers
P. O. Box LG 358
Legon, Accra, Ghana

Tel; 0302-233371
Email: saharanp@africaonline.com

First edition
Copyright © 2012 by   Kathleen O'Brien Wicker
                              Kofi Asare Opoku
                              Margaret Naiandrina Streetor

ISBN 978-9988--647-00-1

All rights reserved. No part of this publication may be reproduced, stored in a retrieval system, or transmitted, in any form or by any means, without the prior written permission of the publisher, nor be otherwise circulated in any form of binding or cover other than that in which it is published and without a similar condition being imposed on the subsequent purchaser.

Cover photo by Kathleen O'Brien Wicker
Frontispiece photo by John Kobina Asmah
Cover design by Franklyn L. Darko

Typeset by Franklyn L. Darko

Dedication

To the late Prophet Jenasman Kwadwo Amoaforo,
Senior Superintendent Prophet of
the Musama Disco Christo Church,
1922-2006

Contents

Foreword   Prophet Moknajeeba Fiifi   vii
                     Jehu-Appiah, General Head
                     Prophet of the Musama Disco
                     Christo Church

Preface   viii

A Word on the Sources   xi

Chapter One   The Life of Prophet Jenasman   1
                     Kwadwo Amoaforo, Senior
                     Superintendent Prophet of the
                     Musama Disco Christo Church.

Chapter Two   The Angels and Mehu   22

Chapter Three   Healing and Ritual   41

Chapter Four   Prophecy   59

Chapter Five   Theology   81

Afterword   98

Foreword

Healing and Prophecy at Mehu is a trophy to the Musama church, and I deem it a privilege to be providing this foreword.

With remarkable depth and clarity, its authors, whose authority springs from outstanding credentials and long-standing association with Mehu, write about the evolution of the individual talent and mission of the founder of Mehu Retreat Centre.

The book sets out not only to discuss the unique ministry of Prophet Jenasman Kwadwo Amoaforo, but also implicitly gives us timeless pathways towards intimacy with God:
    i.   Living in utter simplicity
    ii. Seeking the face of God through prayer and fasting
    iii. Responding with compassion to the needs of others, and
    iv. Yielding completely to the promptings of the spirit.

As *Healing and Prophecy at Mehu* makes clear, for Prophet Amoaforo, access to the "vital hiatus" to borrow a phrase by poet Ruth Fainlight, was mainly inner-directed, being a gift he came to the world with. But the rest of us may take cues from what we learn about him in this book and strive for, or rather surrender to, the grace that makes it possible for one to "seek those things which are above" (Colossians 3:1) with all of one's might, mind and spirit.

Prophet Amoaforo had his peculiar take on some points regarding the spiritual realm, but I am most happy that these three eminently qualified authors have brought his light and example to the top of the lampstand by means of this book.

Prophet Amoaforo, iconoclastic and unblushingly otherworldly, would perhaps have been brushed under the bushel after his death, especially in our time when it is so fashionable to run every hint of the awesome, local or supernatural out of town.

I am sure even those who had the chance to sit at the feet of the tellurian man of Senchi's Mehu will gain fresh insights into Jenasman, fascinating Master of Thunder, most wild-hearted of men, by reading this candid, profound and sympathetic examination of his vision and mission.

Prophet Moknajeeba Jehu-Appiah

Preface

In 1994, an unexpected change in plans permitted us to bring a small group of scholars attending the African Literature Association meeting in Accra to the Mehu Healing and Retreat Centre at Senchi in the Eastern Region of Ghana. That day, we met with Prophet Jenasman Kwadwo Amoaforo, the Senior Superintendent Prophet, and also with his assistant, Madam Margaret Naiandrina Streetor, the Musama Disco Christo Church Pastor at Mehu, Rev. A. K. Mensah, and others. We were also given a tour of the spectacular shrine complex at Mehu and we learned about the rituals conducted there.

All those who had the good fortune to join us in visiting Mehu that day were impressed by the work of Prophet Amoaforo and the elaborate healing shrine he had constructed. But none were more impressed than we were. We decided to ask the Prophet if he would permit us to document the rituals and other religious events held at Mehu during one of the annual anniversary celebrations, and also to allow us and our team to interview him extensively. We wanted to document his life and work as part of our Project, Priesthood and Ritual in Ghana, on the religious and spiritual history of Ghana. The Prophet agreed, and the interviews that began in 1995 continued until the Prophet's death in 2006.

Our work was facilitated from the beginning to the present by the invaluable assistance of Madam Streetor. She transcribed our interviews, provided generous assistance in making all the relevant Mehu documents available to us, and edited our work over the years. We owe her an overwhelming debt of gratitude.

Thanks to the skill of our team videographer, John Kobina Asmah, formerly of the African Studies Institute at the University of Ghana, the 10th Mehu Anniversary Celebration in 1997 was documented. Mr. Asmah also accompanied us on many trips to visit Prophet Amoaforo at Mehu. Mr. Asmah and Kathleen O'Brien Wicker provided the selection of photographs that are included in the volume.

In 2000, Opoku and Wicker published a major article about

Prophet Amoaforo and Mehu in the volume *African Americans and the Bible: Sacred Texts and Social Textures* (New York and London: Continuum) edited by Vincent L. Wimbush. Now, with this new volume, the Project brings to fruition our commitment to the Prophet to publish a book that would document his life, work and spiritual teachings. We discussed the details of this book with Prophet Amoaforo before his passing and he approved our work. Our only regret is that he did not live to see its publication.

This volume contains a Foreword by the new Prophet and Head of the Musama Disco Christo Church, Prophet Moknajeeba Fiifi Jehu-Appiah, a Preface and A Word on the Sources, five chapters discussing Prophet Amoaforo's life and work, and an Afterword.

Chapter I contains a summary of the life of Prophet Amoaforo. The subsequent chapters address different aspects of the Prophet's work. Chapter II focuses on Prophet Amoaforo's unique personal relationship with the angels, how he worked with them at Mehu and the results of that work. Chapter III examines the Prophet's work as a healer, the rituals he used for healing of diseases of all kinds at Mehu, for which many clients sought him out, and the results of his healing practices. In Chapter IV, the emphasis is on the numerous and varied types of prophecies that Prophet Amoaforo was instructed by the angels to give through the course of his lifetime. Chapter V on Prophet Amoaforo's theology may fulfill his desire to publish books that would provide spiritual direction for his clients. In this chapter, we highlight Prophet Amoaforo's creative systematic theology that combines traditional Akan views, mainline Christian beliefs and practices, and his own exceptional spiritual experiences. The "Afterword" offers reflections on the meaning of Prophet Amoaforo's life and work.

An experienced member of our research team, the late Mr. Kwadwo Ampom-Darkwa, who for many years worked for the International Centre for African Music and Dance at the University of Ghana, interviewed Prophet Amoaforo on a number of occasions and produced a record of his research. Mr. Ntow Fiako and Dr. Nicholas Amponsah also assisted us at various times in the interview and translation process.

Mr. K. Osei-Bonsu, Institute of African Studies, also deceased,

Preface

provided valuable service as a typist for the Project, as did Mrs. Nancy S. Burson and Mrs. Rebecca Ballinger, both of Scripps College in Claremont, CA, USA. Mr. Martin Nyamuah, who currently serves as Madam Streetor's assistant, has been invaluable to her and to us in helping to edit the manuscript and in facilitating our work with Madam Streetor. Thanks are due as well to the proofreader and staff at Sub-Saharan Press, and to Ms. Katie Van Heest of Tweed Editing in Seattle, Washington.

Special recognition and thanks go to the former President of Scripps College, Nancy Y. Bekavac, who generously supported our vision with her own enthusiasm. Deans of Faculty and the Treasurer at Scripps College also facilitated our work at Mehu, for which we express appreciation. Funding for the Project until 2003 was provided by Scripps College Faculty Research Funds and by research funds made available to the Claremont Colleges from the Hewlett and Irvine Foundations. Research funds were also made available through The Mary W. Johnson and J. Stanley Johnson Professorship in the Humanities endowment.

Finally, we express our thanks to Prophet Amoaforo, Madam Margaret N. Streetor and the Prophet's associates, and to the Pastor and people at the Mehu Healing and Retreat Centre for generously welcoming us to Mehu when we came to interview Prophet Amoaforo and to carry out the video documentation of the 10th Anniversary Celebration in 1997. We are honored that the new Prophet and Head of the Musama Disco Christo Church, Moknajeeba Fiifi Jehu-Appiah, has graciously agreed to write a Foreword to this volume.

As always, our thanks go to Mrs. Akoss Ofori-Mensah, Managing Director of Sub-Saharan Publishers in Accra, Ghana for enabling us to publish this volume, and to Ghana's Former Ambassador to Germany, Mr. Kwame Adusei-Poku, for offering the hospitality of his home at Peduase during the writing of this book.

Kathleen O'Brien Wicker
Kofi Asare Opoku
Margaret N. Streetor
Peduase, Ghana
October 1, 2011

A Word on the Sources

The main sources of information we have had available to us in writing this book have been the numerous hours we spent with Prophet Amoaforo between 1995-2006, and the archives at the Mehu Healing and Retreat Centre at Senchi which were carefully maintained by Madam Margaret Naiandrina Streetor. She worked in collaboration with the Mehu Literature Committee, including at various times Futaha Kwasi Myles, Suma Kupa Jehu-Appiah, Hutahoba K. Agyei, M.L.K. Jehu-Appiah, K. Buckman and Kryoma Aforo, former Personal Secretary to Prophet Amoaforo, and also with the Musama Disco Christo Church Literature Committee. We are grateful for the use of the extensive archives of the Mehu Healing and Retreat Centre at Senchi in writing this book.

Most of the archived documents at Mehu do not have an attributed author or editor. The Mehu publications that are attributed to specific authors or editors include:

- S. K. Jehu-Appiah. *The Prophetic Ministry of Jenasman K. Amoaforo, 1987;* revised by the Mehu Literature Committee in 1998.
- M. Naiandrina Streetor, Hutahoba K. Agyei, Suma Kupa Jehu-Appiah, eds, *Mehu and the Musama Disco Christo Church, 1996.*
- M. Naiandrina Streetor, ed., *Prophecies* by Prophet Jenasman Kwadwo Amoaforo, 1997; revised in 1998.

Professor Kofi Asare Opoku's writings on the Musama Disco Christo Church have provided valuable background on this Church, of which Prophet Amoaforo was a distinguished member.

- K. A. Opoku, "Changes within Christianity: The Case of the Musama Disco Christo Church," in *Christianity in Independent Africa*, ed., E. Fashole-Luke, Richard Gray, Adrian Hastings, Gordon Tasie (London: Rex Collins) 1978.
- K. A. Opoku, "Musama: the First Seventy-Five Years," a soon to be published manuscript.
- K. A. Opoku, *West African Traditional Religion* (Accra: FEP International Private Limited) 1978.

A Word on the Sources

Mr. K. Ampom-Darkwa's study, *Mehu and Prophet Jenasman Kwadwo Amoaforo (A Documentation)* was published by The Institute of African Studies, University of Ghana, Legon, 1999.

Kofi Asare Opoku and Kathleen O'Brien Wicker published an article on Prophet Amoaforo and Mehu entitled, "The Mehu Healing and Retreat Centre in Ghana," in *African Americans and the Bible: Sacred Texts and Social Structures*, ed. Vincent Wimbush (New York: Continuum) 2000. The Priesthood and Ritual in Ghana Project produced a video entitled *10th Mehu Anniversary Celebration, 1987-1997*.

We have drawn freely from the archival material at Mehu, but we have used quotation marks in the text only when it is clear, either directly or in context, that the material is attributable to Prophet Amoaforo.

The reader should be aware in reading this volume that Prophet Jenasman Amoaforo used the word Mehu in several different ways: 1) Mehu, or the 'Heavenly Mehu' above Heaven, the ultimate destination of souls who had reached their full human development; 2) 'little Mehu', one of the healing centres established by Prophet Amoaforo before the establishment of Mehu at Senchi; 3) 'Mehu', the total complex developed by Prophet Amoaforo at Senchi; 4) 'the Mehu,' a specific area for rituals within the Mehu complex. The terms 'Heavenly Mehu,' 'little Mehu(s)', 'Mehu' and 'the Mehu' are usually used to distinguish among the various meanings of the word Mehu.

Chapter One

The Life of Prophet Jenasman Kwadwo Amoaforo, Senior Superintendent Prophet of the Musama Disco Christo Church

This is the story of Kwadwo Mensah Amoaforo, later Prophet Jenasman Kwadwo Amoaforo, a rare and remarkably gifted person who was born, lived, worked and died in the Gold Coast/Ghana (1922-2006). To the casual observer, he probably did not seem like a rare or remarkable individual. He was a simple man who wore a plain white jumper and pants and the copper ring of the Musama Disco Christo ("Army of the Cross of Christ") Church. He adopted the red fez worn by Muslims, and he traveled for years in a pair of well-worn sandals around Central and Eastern Ghana carrying out his missionary work for the Musama Disco Christo Church.

Kwadwo Amoaforo finally settled later in his life in the Eastern region of Ghana and established a successful healing shrine of the Musama Disco Christo Church at Senchi called the Mehu Healing and Retreat Centre, where he also worked as a farmer and ran an award-winning tilapia farm. He was witty and garrulous, but he was considered illiterate because he neither spoke nor wrote in English, despite the fact that he was fluent in several local languages.

Kwadwo Amoaforo gave the lie to appearances, however. As a Mensah, a third-born male, who exhibited some exceptional qualities, it was not surprising that he would distinguish himself in some special way. In his case, he became known through his association with the Musama Disco Christo Church. As a missionary of that Church for over sixty years, he established the Church in many areas of Ghana and manifested his exceptional gifts of persuasive preaching, healing miracles, ability to discern and exorcise demons, and prophecy. Throughout his life he had an extraordinary relationship with the angels. His openness to all religious traditions was remarkable, given the sectarian nature of many Christian Churches in Ghana.

The exceptional gifts that Prophet Amoaforo had – healing, powerful preaching, exorcism, and astral travel – were considered by the Musama Church, the Mehu community and others as spiritual gifts. Prophet Amoaforo himself considered them gifts of the angels. More recently, such gifts are considered human capacities that only a limited number of people have been able to access, especially to the extent and with the facility that Prophet Amoaforo demonstrated. So, indirectly at least, they should still be regarded as spiritual gifts.

Kwadwo Amoaforo evolved in such extraordinary ways during his lifetime that by the end of his life he could claim to be an "ascended master," someone who had developed spiritually to the point that he no longer had to be reincarnated after death to complete his life contract with God. He also regarded himself as an angel in human form.

Kwadwo Amoaforo began life in the ordinary way, but perhaps it was not all that ordinary after all. Kwadwo's parents were the late Geoffrey Kwadwo Amoaforo and the late Madam Alice Afua Agyaakobea from the Amoakaade Aboradze clan of Gyakiti in the Akwamu district in the Eastern Region of the Gold Coast, now Ghana. They had settled at Sesaman near Asesewa in the Krobo area of the country. When his mother conceived for the third time, having lost two other children already, she must have had some anxiety about the outcome of this pregnancy. Kwadwo's father, a Presbyter of the Presbyterian Church, slept in the church at night during this period, praying ceaselessly to God to avert his mishap and give him a child. Whether Kwadwo's birth was the outcome of a natural process or God's answer to their prayers, or both, on the 4th of April, 1922, Kwadwo Mensah was born at Sesaman.

Among the stories told about Kwadwo's early years, there was one that presaged Kwadwo's extraordinary future. One day, he disappeared as a young baby from the family's thatched house in Sesaman around one o'clock in the morning. His mother discovered he was not in bed and reported this to her husband. He blamed the mother for her lack of vigilance, but she in turn accused him of the same. Then they heard the cry of a baby in a nearby forest and the father went out to find Kwadwo lying in the bush.

The next morning around 11:00 in the morning, a Muslim Al-Haji from Togo came to the family cottage and said: "You have given birth to a little boy. This boy is going to do a great deal of work in all parts of the world." Then the Al-Haji looked at Kwadwo and said, "This is the child I am talking about." The father dismissed the Al-Haji from the house, fearing that he had been the abductor.

According to the Prophet later in life, he was abducted by the demon Lucifer himself who had stolen him from the home and taken him to the forest. These different versions of the story are not contradictory, however. The second version is a theological interpretation of events rather than an historical version. Such theological narratives express what is called "Divine Man" theology, and is intended to help listeners see the larger significance of events in the life of an apparently unremarkable person who later proves to be an extraordinary individual.

Over time Kwadwo's parents learned more about their son's special abilities through other experiences as well. When Kwadwo was four years old, he asked his father to get him a red fez worn by Muslims, and he continued to wear the fez throughout his life. The hat may have presaged the openness to all religions that characterized his life and work. A photograph of young Kwadwo wearing a fez was taken by an American photographer whom children in the area called *"kura mankyese,"* meaning "match holder" from the matchbox he shook when taking photographs to gain the attention of the children.

Several other incidents were also reported that witnessed to the unusual character of the young Kwadwo Amoaforo. When he was a youth, it was said that everything he predicted came true. At Frankadua in 1938, he had a pet bird that sang beautifully. One day when Kwadwo was sent to run some errands, the bird flew away. He was very sad about this, but he told his father that the bird would come back within two weeks. On the midnight of the stipulated time, he saw the bird flying from west to east. Then he heard a voice telling him that the bird was coming. Next morning he got some grains and water ready and put them in the bird's cage, leaving the cage door open. Kwadwo then told his father that he would be waiting for his bird and did not want to do any errands that day. By 11:00 that morning the bird returned, made its usual noise and entered the cage. Kwadwo closed the door of the cage and was very happy with his pet, a confirmation of his prediction to his father.

In another incident, young Kwadwo was sitting with his parents and some relatives at a meal in Gyakiti when he saw a policeman coming. A voice told him that the policeman was going to arrest his uncle, Kwaku Mamfe, who was also at the meal. Kwadwo told his uncle to run away, but he was severely beaten for saying such a thing. About five minutes later, the policeman arrived to arrest his uncle for the Akwamufie Chief's palace because of some offence he had committed.

Kwadwo had to give up his education at primary four due to an acute stomach ailment. His father took him to receive medical attention at Kpalime in what was then Togoland. His father was directed to a French doctor there by a Togolese farmer who worked in the Krobo area. After receiving treatment for a month at Kpalime, he was completely cured and father and son returned to the Gold Coast.

On their return, Kwadwo stayed with his father at Frankadua to help him run his shop. Though Kwadwo was the only child at the time (he had a sister later in life), he was not pampered or spoiled. He was taught by his parents, especially his mother, to work hard. Having stayed with his father for some time, Kwadwo decided to learn a trade, so he left for Koforidua near Asesewa in the Eastern Region to become an apprentice to one Mr. Addo, a tailor, following the direction of a spiritual voice he heard in 1938/39. In the 1940's, when he was an apprentice tailor at Koforidua, he had to run errands and do odd jobs in his spare time to earn pocket money. Eventually Kwadwo became a well-established tailor with three sewing machines (a Vestor, an Adler and a Singer) and seven apprentices.

An event of significance occurred in Kwadwo's life shortly after he moved to Koforidua to become an apprentice tailor. The Musama Disco Christo Church was being introduced there by missionaries who came to the area. When the Musama preachers arrived where

Kwadwo lived, many people became excited. Kwadwo was not impressed by these preachers, but it was soon reported that the brother of a pastor named Selby regained his sight when the Musama people prayed and touched his face, and that attracted the notice of the people.

Soon thereafter, Kwadwo himself became involved in the healing of his master's wife, who had been unable to conceive for two years. He had no idea how or why it had happened, a statement that intuitives also make about the source of their capacities. This experience led to his conversion to the Musama Disco Christo Church. Later, Kwadwo said that during those days he had the feeling that the angels of God were always with him, watching over him.

After joining the Musama Church at Koforidua and becoming a missionary, Kwadwo, who was then about twenty years old, was told to fast for ninety days. He had encounters with angels, two of whom he identified as *Helasaliza* and *Halbasak*. During the Koforidua period, he said, he felt that the angels had, metaphorically, put a heavy "spiritual engine" into his stomach and spiritual "copper wires" in his arms and legs, and he developed into a spiritually strong person.

"Spiritual engine" and "copper wires" were Prophet Amoaforo's attempt to use human language to express what were essentially spiritual experiences. Though some people, upon meeting Prophet Amoaforo, thought they could see evidence of an engine in his stomach, it is more likely that a metaphorical rather than an actual engine empowered him.

The angels also took the Prophet under the Volta River for three days where they prepared him for his mission. He said that some of his powers were hidden in that river so that his enemies would not be able to find them.

Word of Kwadwo's activities reached the Head of the Musama Disco Christo Church, Prophet Jemisimiham Jehu-Appiah, through the reports of missionaries. Accordingly, he asked them to go back and look for the young man that they told him about and bring him back to old Mozano (Fomena), where his headquarters were located. They found Kwadwo and returned with him from Abodom to Mozano.

Kwadwo had been in Fomena for about a week when the Prophet

sent for him. Akaboha Jehu-Appiah I told Kwadwo that he had received a revelation from God that, after the death of the outstanding Musama Disco Christo Church Prophet Boaz, another prophet would emerge from the Eastern Region who would complete the building of the Musama Church. The Akaboha believed Kwadwo Amoaforo would be that prophet, and said to him, "If you are the great one sent to us by God, then we are blessed."

Later, Kwadwo and the Akaboha I, Jemisimiham Jehu-Appiah, met at Fomena in the bush at 1:00 in the morning. Kwadwo reported that they talked for quite a long time. He stated later in life as he recounted this incident: "The Akaboha told me that the battle that was to be fought for Africa was great, so I should team up with him to fight together for victory. If we were to fight individually or separately, the struggle would be much harder." The Akaboha invited Kwadwo to become his right hand man and Kwadwo agreed to it.

Then the Akaboha told Kwadwo about God's plan to send him on a missionary journey to do his work. Subsequently, in 1943, the Akaboha anointed Kwadwo, ordained him as a Junior Prophet and gave him the heavenly name "Jenasman" which means "master of the angels who produce thunder". The Akaboha also established Kwadwo in his own family so that he would not break away from him in the future, since Kwadwo came from a different ethnic group. The Akaboha gave his wife's niece, Mameeda Abena Asantewa, to be married to Jenasman in the future. They remained married until Prophet Amoaforo's death.

Jenasman's mother supported the idea of his engagement with the Musama Church and the Akaboha's family, but his father was against it. He thought Kwadwo would have many enemies who would try to kill him because they were jealous of his gifts, and because Jenasman was an Akwamu but the Musama Disco Christo Church people were Gomoas. Kwadwo ignored his father's advice and continued to do God's work in the Musama Disco Christo Church. As for being an Akwamu in a Fante community, Jenasman commented, "I just pretend and try to co-habit with them, having gone through hard times as a result of their maltreatment and actions…The relationship is there. I do not force issues on them to respect me."

The Christianity that Kwadwo Amoaforo was introduced to in

the Musama Disco Christo Church was quite different from the Christianity that was brought to the Gold Coast (Ghana) as early as the late 15th century by Europeans. It also differed from that of the later 19th century missionaries to the Gold Coast who established schools and clinics to aid in their evangelistic mission and, in their view, to benefit the colonized people. Kwadwo's parents were devout Presbyterians and quite likely Christians in the 19th century missionary tradition, but it seems that young Kwadwo Amoaforo probably had only a minimal exposure to these missionaries and pastors.

Thanks to his encounter with Akaboha I, Jemisimiham Jehu-Appiah and the Musama Disco Christo Church, Kwadwo became part of an independent or indigenous Christian tradition launched by Africans who wanted to belong to an African Christian Church rather than a European Christian Church. These indigenous Christian Churches both reinterpreted traditional culture and responded to the problems created by missionary Christianity. The Musama Disco Christo Church and other indigenous Christian Churches created a new type of African Christianity that transformed colonial Christianity into a religion not of creed and conformity to Western tenets and practices, but one that sought the total well-being of adherents in their daily lives as Africans.

The Musama Disco Christo Church regarded itself as an African Church that had received a special revelation from God through its founder and his successors as to the nature of the Christianity that Africans were intended to believe in and to practice. The Church maintained an indigenous clergy in leadership positions, and reinterpreted Christian teachings and practices to bring them more into line with traditional cultural beliefs and practices.

Catechist Joseph William Egyanka Appiah, the founder, understood the significance of combining traditional cultural ideas and practices with Christian missionary teaching, thanks to a revelation he had in 1916. In 1919, he initiated a prayer group in the local Methodist Church at Gomoa Ogwan in the Central Region of the Gold Coast where he was a member. That prayer group later became known as the Faith Society (*Egyedzifo Kuw*). They practised speaking in tongues, faith healing and laying on of hands as important parts of their work and practice.

The Methodist Church, however, became suspicious of the activities of the Faith Society and expelled the members from their Church. Shortly after their dismissal from the Methodist Church in 1922, the Faith Society became known as the Musama Disco Christo Church through a revelation to the founder, J.W.E. Appiah, who was given the "heavenly name" Jemisimiham Jehu-Appiah, also through revelation.

His wife, Hannah Barnes, who had also been given special spiritual gifts, became known as Prophetess Nathalomoa Jehu-Appiah. Their first child, Kwesi Nyamekye, born on August 24, 1924, was given the revealed name Matapoly Moses Jehu-Appiah, and was prophesied to become the next Akaboha and build the Church further.

The Musama Disco Christo Church claimed that *Jehu* was the name of the angel who was commissioned to fill all the requests of the Faith society as well as the angel who appeared to Moses in a flame of fire. Ex. 3:2 refers to an unnamed angel of the Lord. Some interpret this being as Yahweh; the Musama Disco Christo Church considers it an angelic being named *Jehu*. The angel *Jehu*, as well as a multitude of other angels, were to continue to play an important role in the life of the new Prophet Jenasman Amoaforo and in the Mehu Healing and Retreat Centre that Prophet Amoaforo would establish later in his life.

As part of his missionary work, Prophet Amoaforo established Musama Disco Christo Church stations in many places in the Gold Coast. He also visited them from time to time to supervise and revive the weak stations. According to Prophet Amoaforo, the mission of the Musama Disco Christo Church was threefold: to preach the true gospel of the unity of all religions, all races and nations; to heal diseases of all kinds; and to protect and deliver people from the destructive forces of the devil and other demonic spirits, in heaven, on earth, under the earth, and in the sea.

In his work, Prophet Amoaforo healed hundreds of people from ailments natural and spiritual: barrenness, madness, bodily burns, fits and peculiar diseases difficult to classify. Healing was considered an important part of the mission of the Musama Disco Christo Church from the beginning, since the Church considered healing as the most effective means of evangelization.

Jenasman spent twelve years at Koforidua, during which time he purchased land for a Church building with the help of Messrs. Asma and Koomson. He also exposed talismans and amulets possessed by some elders of the Church at Effiduase, Koforidua and explained that it was against Church rules for members to possess them. Then he moved to Nsawam to continue the work of God. From Nsawam he supervised the Church work in Accra and Suhum.

In a small village between Nsawam and Adeiso he met a man named Mr. Lamptey who had extraordinary powers of healing, treating infertility and madness, and divining the future through the use of a magic stone from India and a ring that he placed on top of the stone. Mr. Lamptey could even predict when a person would die.

One day, Jenasman decided to visit Mr. Lamptey in the guise of a homeless man. When Mr. Lamptey inquired about his occupation, Jenasman said he was a palm wine tapper, a job for rural, low status people. Surprised, Mr. Lamptey said Jenasman was one of the greatest philosophers in the world and he thought Jenasman should be doing something better. So Mr. Lamptey invited Jenasman to move into his house in order to work with him to develop his gifts.

Mr. Lamptey made a number of prophecies about Jenasman's remarkable future, including that he would travel widely doing wonderful work, and that he would finally settle somewhere near the Volta River. He noted also that Jenasman would be transferred from Nsawam to a new place that was close to a river. That place, presumably, was Swedru where he lived by a riverside for a time.

From Swedru Prophet Amoaforo supervised Winneba, Cape Coast, Asafo, Nsabaa, Nkum, Nyakrom, Akroso and Bobikuma. During this time, a Mr. Hagan was helpful to him. His mission in Swedru lasted seven years. He had more than 600 followers in his mission at Swedru. While he was there, the late Akwamuhene, Nana Kwafo Akoto, sent some messengers to come for him because Nana felt his services were more needed in the Akwamu area than in Fanteland where he was based.

In the Eastern Region, Prophet J. K. Amoaforo established the Church at Asesewa, Akroso, Akushia, Nkumankua, Ayesu, Anyebone, Bisa, Kpongunor, Nnuaso and Kpong, all in the Krobo area. He also worked at New Juaben, Tinkong, Larteh, Bekoe Akuraa and Coaltar.

With valuable assistance from Rev. Selby, Jenasman also established the Church at Gyakiti, Akwamufie, Anum, Boso, Asikuma, Aboasa, Akosombo, Enyensu, and Mpakadan.

In the Brong Ahafo Region, Jenasman established the Church at Goaso, Ahafoano, Sunyani, Asuoho and Kyiraa. In Greater Accra, he established the Church at Chorkor, Kokomlemle, Airport, and Post Office with the help of Messrs. Sackey and Nyarkotey.

In the Asante Region, Jenasman established the Church at Mbromu, Kumasi, Tafo, Santaase, Suame, Asokore, Effiduase, Ejisu, Juaben, Juaso, Ntumkum, Seniagya and Asante Mampong with the help of Messrs. Boampong, Boateng and Manu.

In the Volta Region, Jenasman established the Church at Pareman, Peki, Kpeve, Kpando, Hoviepe, Ho, Borada, Jasikan, Worawora, Abotoase and Hohoe.

The effectiveness of Prophet Amoaforo's preaching was confirmed by his many converts and by demonstrations of God's power through exorcisms, healings and prophecies.

An extraordinary story of the Prophet's power as an exorcist comes from Hoviepe in the Volta area where Prophet Amoaforo encountered a man who had killed some forty-nine people by nailing up a string while invoking a person's name. This ritual would drag the one whose name was mentioned to him to be hacked to pieces in the forest, and then he took the victim's blood to his local divinity as a sacrifice. All the citizens were afraid of the man because of his clandestine, brutal activities. When Prophet Amoaforo demonstrated no fear of the man or of going into the forest, however, the man repented and became a member of the Musama Disco Christo Church.

On another occasion, Jenasman was invited to Lome in Togo to assist fishermen in getting a good catch. He reported that he talked to the spirits in the sea to grant the wish of the fishermen, and their wish was granted. Then fishermen from Ada Foah and Cotonou in Benin also made the same request of him, with the same result. The fishermen in Cotonou were surprised that the Prophet did not use ritual objects, such as those sold in the fetish market in Cotonou and used by the spiritualists there, but the Prophet told them it was the "spiritual engine" that had been placed in his stomach that made it possible for him to do this.

Prophet Amoaforo's remarkable prophetic powers were also demonstrated in the Akwamu area of Ghana, where he went in response to divine guidance. For several generations, the Akwamu people had not prospered. They were thought to have been cursed by the Asante counselor and prophet, Okomfo Anokye. It was said that when Okomfo Anokye visited the Akwamu people from Awukugua, they did not give him due recognition because he was not a royal and they tried to kill him. He managed to escape, however, and in his wrath he delivered a curse that even though the Akwamu lived by the mighty River Volta, they would never prosper and would live in dust. Hence, the Akwamu had always attributed their poor situation to Anokye's curse.

Despite the fabled curse of Okomfo Anokye however, Jenasman had a vision that he himself was going to receive some special spiritual power to help build Africa and this area in particular. In addition, he had already been invited by Akwamuhene Nana Kwafo Akoto, to come to Akwamu. So, accompanied by Messers. Otchere Debra and E.C. Appiah, he crossed the Volta by canoe and arrived at Akwamufie.

Prophet Amoaforo reported to the Akwamuhene, Nana Kwafo Akoto, that he had made an astral journey into space, and on one occasion he came into contact with an unusual star that had a distinctive musical beat, a beat that Jenasman often demonstrated for his hearers. He was informed that the star was called Dominita and he was told by the angels that he should bring that star in the form of a spiritual monument to the Akwamu people so that they could prosper and become a great, healthy nation numbering millions.

It took a full year before Nana Kwafo Akoto, Paramount Chief of the Akwamu Traditional Area, decided to accept this spiritual gift and for the angels to communicate with the Prophet. In 1947, Prophet Amoaforo began building the monument named Makatapi at Akwamufie in a location established by divination. The structure was dedicated in 1951. He prophesied that the Makatapi would make Akwamu an "Eye of God" in the Gold Coast, that it would bring many jobs to the area, that the Gold Coast would win its independence from Britain, and that the new nation would be led by the Dominita star.

The Prophet also indicated that the Akosombo Hydroelectric Project would be built in the area. This would bring an increase in commerce and cause an influx of new residents. Finally, he designated the place where the Volta River would be bridged at Atimpoku, to the benefit of the inhabitants of the area and of Ghana.

An unfortunate event occurred during the construction of the Akosombo dam, however. Jenasman was imprisoned at Nsawam for forgery committed by a bank manager conducting business on his behalf, and in 1963/64, he was sentenced to jail for seven years. However, he won an appeal after serving four years and was acquitted and discharged. His mother died while he was in prison.

In 1979, Prophet Amoaforo was given the difficult task of prophetically condemning Miritaiah Jonah Jehu-Appiah, Akaboha III, for violating God's precepts and he predicted the Akaboha's removal from his position in the Musama Disco Christo Church. As a result, Prophet Amoaforo himself was removed by the Church from his position as Prophet and healer. Even though he knew he was unjustly condemned, he accepted this punishment until it was withdrawn by Akaboha III in 1985.

In the same year, 1985, Prophet Amoaforo undertook a two year and seven month fast. According to his account, he was inspired by the angels to undertake the fast. The fast prepared him to establish the Mehu Healing and Retreat Centre at Senchi Ferry in the Eastern Region of Ghana. Mehu at Senchi was constructed architecturally according to the visions Prophet Amoaforo had in the spiritual realm during his astral travels. It was also based on some designs that the angels had told him to record during his period as a tailor.

Prophet Amoaforo had many difficulties spiritually and financially in his efforts to establish Mehu. The Musama Disco Christo Church did not offer monetary support for the construction. Some in the Church took a 'wait and see' attitude with regard to Mehu. But contributions from well-wishers and clients and gifts to the Prophet helped to defray the costs. Finally the first structures that formed the basis of Mehu were completed and Mehu was officially dedicated on June 28, 1987 by the Akaboha III, General Head of the Musama Disco Christo Church, as the Mehu Healing and Retreat Centre.

Between 1987 and 2000, Prophet Amoaforo also fasted to construct other monuments at Mehu. The Nuhu/Kimakaro, the dwelling of the angel *Habu* that contained the star of prosperity, was followed by the Victory Stone in May, 1990. The Big Cross, Huma, was constructed in 1992, and the Helobim, a big star, was erected in the year 2000. A monument to the *Helalalalaahu* Shepherds, angels who resided on the 25th planet, followed after that and also one showing a hand raised, and the inscription "Africa has lifted her hand". Each of these structures had a specific spiritual function in the systems the Prophet directed people to carry out at Mehu.

The design and significance of the structures as well as the theological message of the wall paintings at Mehu will be discussed later in this book, as will the rituals and practices that Prophet Amoaforo conducted at the shrine, and the powerful healing record the Prophet achieved at Mehu. All of these topics deserve and will receive more than the passing mention they are given in this overview of Prophet Jenasman Amoaforo's life and work.

Toward the end of his long and fruitful life, the Prophet's health began to fail. In 2002, the Akaboha III informed Prophet Amoaforo that his friend, Dr. Mills, at the local hospital wanted him to come for an examination. The doctor told him that his blood pressure was high and gave him medications for this and other problems.

The Prophet also explained that the angels had healed him in the astral world. He said that one night he saw himself being put on a stretcher by five angels and taken to the 12th planet where the angels, *Humala*, *Omala*, *Famala*, *Nyamfala* and *Fala*, treated him. He said, metaphorically, "they used their instruments on my body which was like fire". When the angels were finished treating Prophet Amoaforo, they sent him back to the earthly planet to live out his final days.

The Prophet said that these angels knew that he was very ill because the clouds around him were very thick and heavy. When he arrived in the astral realm he got fire energy and strength to be able to cope with the situation, so that he could continue to operate. The people at Mehu, however, were quite afraid that something fatal was going to happen to him and they wanted him to rest in bed, but "within a twinkle he was sitting under the mango tree as usual."

A few years later, Prophet Amoaforo was hospitalized for ten days at the Volta River Authority Hospital at Akosombo due to a stomach upset. After that, he visited an eye specialist for treatment of glaucoma from time to time. Then bodily rashes set in with sores on some parts of his body. On January 17, 2006, he called in a few people he was close to, including his wife and daughter, Rev. Mensah the Pastor, Madam Streetor and Prophet Omaya and told them that his time on this planet was coming to an end. He said he was on a waiting list to be taken away. After that he thanked them and advised them to work hard. He, too, continued his own hard work for the duration of his life.

From then on, Prophet Amoaforo was ill periodically. He managed to endure until the middle of June, 2006 when the situation worsened. He was then taken to the hospital with the hope that he would be admitted and treated there. Instead, however, Prophet Amoaforo was given medicine and told to go home. From then on, he was in a coma for two weeks. He passed away on Friday, June 30, 2006 about twelve noon. He ordered that, following his death, the hearths should be kept burning for seven days, and that prayers be said for him for fourteen days, morning and evening.

Prophet Amoaforo's funeral was held at Mehu from Friday, September 29 to Sunday October 1, 2006. Prophet Jenasman Kwadwo Amoaforo, Senior Superintendent Prophet of the Musama Disco Church at Senchi Ferry was then buried with his stone in his hand, according to his request, in a tomb at Mehu that had been specially prepared for him. At the time of his death, he was 84 years old.

Prophet Amoaforo once described the roles he saw himself playing at Mehu as "healing all sorts of spiritual diseases; establishing a crop farm and fish pond on the compound of the Healing Camp at Senchi for the benefit of the community; prophesying; uniting all religions and races of all nations and bringing them together to realize the Universal Brotherhood of Mankind". Looking back over his life, it becomes clear that he worked untiringly to achieve those goals, and that he did achieve them in a most remarkable way.

The Home Mission Board of the Musama Disco Christo Church offered the following tribute to the memory of Prophet Jenasman Amoaforo on the occasion of his burial and funeral service, September 29-October 1, 2006:

"Prophet Jenasman Kwadwo Amoaforo was born in 1922. However it was in 1940 that his membership of the Musama Disco Christo Church started. At a crusade organized by the Church in Koforidua, Prophet Jenasman was instructed by the Holy Spirit to heal a woman who had been pregnant for two (2) years. He followed this experience with a 90 day fast after which the Lord used him to perform many miracles.

"As a consecrated worker of the Musama Disco Christo Church, Prophet Jenasman Amoaforo was first stationed at Koforidua. He was ordained a Junior Prophet in 1943 by the Akaboha I. Thus until his death he was the only surviving Prophet ordained by the founder of the Musama Disco Christo Church.

"While at his last station, Swedru, he prophesied the future prosperity of Akwamu to include the fact that it would become the 'Eye' of the then Gold Coast. He also indicated the exact spot where the bridge over the Volta was to be built. His prophecies about Akwamu came to pass with the building of the bridge at the spot he had indicated. Indeed with the building of Akosombo Dam, Akwamu became the "Eye" of Ghana.

"Prophet Jenasman Amoaforo started the Healing and Retreat Centre at Senchi in 1987. The Lord used Prophet Jenasman Amoaforo to perform many spiritual and physical feats. But he will be remembered for one significant prophecy which he gave in 1979. This prophecy which predicted the dismissal from office of the Akaboha III of the Musama Disco Christo Church came to pass, with events which culminated in the leadership crisis in the Church since 2003.

"With his call into eternity, the Musama Disco Christo Church has lost one of her greatest prophets. May the Lord grant him eternal rest. Amen."

An eloquent tribute was also prepared by Madam Margaret Naiandrina Streetor, Prophet Amoaforo's faithful assistant and loyal friend:

"My association with the Prophet, which began forty-two years ago when he healed me of a spiritual disease, has afforded me the opportunity to know some of his qualities.

"He was humble and modest despite the great power in him. He joked with all levels of people, even children. I was disturbed initially about it when I got closer because of this work. When you were doing serious business with him, he would cut in to joke on some trivial matter with someone passing by. I held him in high esteem, so I questioned him about it.

"He explained that he had a very great power and light within him, and it would ward off people if he were not mellow. The following are a few slogans he shared with people he joked with. *Odii* – short form of *Odiyifo,* meaning Prophet (Twi), *Mekuu* – short form of *Mekudi* (Hausa) meaning money, *Adi* – (Twi) meaning it worked, also the same as *Aye Adwuma* (Twi).

"His commitment was to fulfill the mission that brought him to this planet, no matter the cost. His mission was to save those Satan had put in bondage and to prepare souls for heaven. He worked towards those goals even though it might cost him his life. Physically, he had the general welfare of people at heart. He saw to people's needs materially, feeding and healing them and improving their lives.

"His faith in God was very strong. During difficulties and life's storms he knew his God would intervene. This was demonstrated when he was imprisoned at Nsawam for forgery because of the actions of a bank manager who operated on his behalf. He prayed steadfastly and worked on an appeal at the court. He won the appeal and was acquitted and discharged. His strong faith was also demonstrated in healing. At times when people had given up on some sickness he raised their hopes and healed them. He did not give up when all hope was lost.

"He was very bold. This was demonstrated when he had to deliver the 1979 prophecy for correcting the wrong behaviour going on in the Musama Church, despite the repercussions. It was a bitter pill to swallow. The Head of the Musama Church suspended him for seven years, amidst castigations.

"He was brave. Sometimes people with strange diseases which were frightening were sent to him. People thought they were bad cases, but he handled them to their surprise.

"He was so generous that he borrowed to satisfy the needy when he had nothing to spare. He sacrificed his life and property for the work of God. He shared whatever he had with all. He shared his farm products with all and sundry, including members of Musama Disco Christo Church and non-members.

"He was sympathetic. This was seen in the way he felt for the sick, by the way he handled them, straining himself to heal them. He did not mince words even if it would cost him his life. He did not fear anybody so far as the truth was concerned. He was not selfish. He had a habit of sharing what he had, as he always said: 'I brought nothing into this world and will take nothing when I am leaving it.'

"What he detested most was cheating. His workers on the farm always cheated him by maligning him and stealing farm products, yet he paid them their full wages and fees. When he was told about the workers' behaviour, his answer was that he preferred to be cheated than to cheat, because the cheaters would pay for it some time.

"The Prophet was a traditionalist who was happy with the old ways of living and doing things. The modern trends did not appeal to him. He did not adopt modern methods of farming, eating and medical treatment, until toward the end of his life, when his health deteriorated and he began accepting medical treatment. He believed strongly in faith healing.

"The only difficulty the Prophet had was his gift of power from God. His father foresaw it and advised him against associating with the group at Gomoa because they would envy his power and would try to kill him.

"The Prophet proved his father right later on in life when the Musama Disco Christo Church treated him severely after he delivered the November, 1979 prophecy about correcting the wrongs in the Church. He was suspended for seven years. After twenty-three years, these wrongs caused a crisis in the Church. The truth came out.

"Secondly, he was accused because he established Mehu in Senchi in the Eastern Region of Ghana, instead of at Mozano. His explanation was that 'God is not worshipped only in Jerusalem. God does what he likes.' The Prophet was a father to all, not only to his biological children and relations. He treated all equally, materially and spiritually. Visitors, petitioners, consultees, the sick and his family members shared accommodation at the centre and products from his farm and fishpond.

"Even though he was an angel, the Prophet had human attributes. He was talkative. He could talk the whole day without getting tired.

"The Prophet's anger matched his name, Jenasman, meaning master of thunder. His anger did not last, though. As soon as he made his point in anger, he came out of it and life continued normally as though nothing had happened. He did not harbour grudges, because he thought that if one harboured grudges, it closed his gate to heaven. When asked about his severe treatment of others when he was annoyed, his explanation was that if he were not so severe, the person might not change immediately. Then he might fall into a trap that would not augur well for him. Another explanation was that developed persons needed to advise persons who thought they were wise that they actually were not.

"His tenacity of purpose was very strong. If he made up his mind to do something, no one could convince him to stop doing it, even if those people knew from their experience that the end result would be negative.

"A clear example is his planting of pepper on the farm that did not have the correct type of soil for it. Even when the Agriculture Extension from the Ministry of Agriculture advised against it, he stuck to his idea and went ahead. All the attempts failed and the pepper projects were failures and resulted in the loss of millions of Cedis.

"But, the Prophet's angelic behaviour outweighed his human weaknesses. His beneficiaries were numerous. Everybody who associated with him benefited either spiritually or physically from him, by way of being healed from sickness, being protected or saved from death, prospering in life and leading a meaningful life.

"The Prophet says that his life should benefit all, since that is the purpose of his being sent to this planet. Thanks be to God for his life."

The Research team from The Institute of African Studies at the University of Ghana, Professor Kofi Asare Opoku, Mr. K. Ampom-Darkwa, Mr. John Asmah, Mr. K. Osei Bonsu, and Mr. Duwonu Normanyo, and Professor Kathleen O'Brien Wicker, Mrs. Nancy Burson and Mrs. Rebecca Ballinger from Scripps College in Claremont, California, also offered the following tribute:

"The passing away of Prophet Jenasman Kwadwo Amoaforo has deprived Ghana, Africa and the whole world of a true man of God, a man with an indomitable tenacity of spirit, and a man who, though he rarely left his usual surroundings, traveled great distances in spiritual journeys and returned with amazing insights and celestial guidance. The paintings and structures at Mehu bear eloquent testimony to his astral experiences.

"We came to know, admire and love Prophet Amoaforo in the course of our researches in connection with our project, *Priesthood and Ritual in Ghana*, in the early part of the 1990's and we consider ourselves immeasurably blessed in being numbered among his friends.

"Prophet Amoaforo welcomed us with open arms when we told him of our research objectives and gave us every assistance in our project, *Healing and Prophecy at Mehu: The life and Work of Prophet Jenasman Kwadwo Amoaforo*. This work is now completed, and it is our hope that it will stand as a lasting testimony to his illustrious memory.

"Prophet Amoaforo lived a good life, a life of simplicity, deep spirituality and faith, a life dedicated to righteousness and justice, to love and peace. Perhaps without knowing, and certainly without saying, Prophet Amoaforo acted as God's child and God's agent, even perhaps as one of God's angels. To us, he became the best of what God made, a true channel of God's peace. He was absolutely selfless, and made people feel that they were the most important persons in the world.

"We remain constantly amazed at the number of people who came to Mehu to see him and recall the compassionate attention he paid to their needs. Prophet Amoaforo certainly became for us the human expression of the Prayer of St. Francis: 'Lord, grant that I may seek rather to comfort than to be comforted, to understand than to be understood, to love rather than to be loved.'

"Despite the many crosses Prophet Amoaforo bore in his life, he never uttered a word of self-pity or doubt. Instead, he remained steadfast till his last breath. He touched each of our lives and his memory is forever etched in our hearts. May the memory of our beloved Prophet Jenasman Kwadwo Amoaforo serve as a source of blessing and inspiration to all who seek to do the same."

In the years after Prophet Amoaforo's death, he manifested himself several times to persons connected with Mehu.

Madam Margaret Naiandrina Streetor also reported that she herself had two such manifestations. "After his death but before his funeral, as I was attacked or entangled with a severe stomach ulcer, I had an encounter with him but his countenance was not revealed. All that I saw was his right hand on the painful part of my stomach and amazingly, I recovered." (July 2006).

"Secondly, I had plans to renovate the Mehu monment so I bought sand and stones and cement. That very night he revealed himself. I saw him standing on an unknown mountain. When he turned back to look at me, He disappeared." (July, 2009)

Madam Streetor also reported: "On another occasion in a state of wrath, the Prophet revealed himself to one Hilcanoda Grace Amenya, a member of the Musama Disco Christo Church at Hohoe, and told her to tell Rev. Andoh that he should quickly move to the Mehu Healing and Retreat Centre at Senchi to rekindle the Prophet's fire. Despite the fact that he had revealed himself on two occasions to Hilcanoda Grace Amenya to deliver this news, he had been unavailing." This occurred in the latter part of 2008.

According to Madam Streetor, Kriyoma Aforo had a revelation of the late Prophet Jenasman Kwadwo Amoaforo sometime later when the late Prophet made the remark that the congregation always complains of poverty and financial constraints. Therefore they should fast and pray for a day, and make an offering that should be shared among four particular people and told to wait upon the Lord for a miracle.

Mary Ampia, who is a member, had a revelation that she had been ill and had come to the Mehu Healing and Retreat Centre where she met the late Prophet sitting with his two legs crossed holding a glowing candle. The late prophet asked the workers to get Mary Ampia bathing water from the Mehu so as to bathe with. Accordingly, she returned after her bath to the Mehu (a site in the Mehu Healing and Retreat Centre) where she saw a mass of people, some sweeping and cleaning, others doing construction works, some doing painting and so on, all these were workers at the Mehu Healing and Retreat Centre. She then asked whether she could also participate in the work and as she picked a broom to sweep, she woke up from her sleep.

With the departure of Miritaiah Jonah Jehu-Appiah, Akaboha III, from the Musama Disco Christo Church headquarters at Mozano in January, 2011, the work of purifying the Musama Disco Christo Church, to which Prophet Amoaforo had dedicated so much of his life, was finally complete.

Chapter Two

The Angels and Mehu

Prophet Jenasman Amoaforo recognized the angels as the source of his power to accomplish his exceptional deeds. In fact, his experiences in the astral realm and with the angels can seem even more amazing than his earthly experiences. Both provide an essential insight into his life.

Prophet Amoaforo undoubtedly learned from the Musama Disco Christo Church and the Bible about the angelic tradition in Judaism and in Christianity. Angels belonged to a higher order of creation than human beings. They did not appear to have a physical nature, but they did have different names and personalities. They interacted with Prophet Amoaforo and guided him throughout his life about what he was supposed to do and how to do it, and their advice almost invariably yielded positive results. Prophet Amoaforo's angelology was more developed and complex than any account in the Bible, thanks to his many encounters with them.

Angels were also familiar to Musama Disco Christo Church members through the history and traditions of the Church. During the early days of the Faith Society, precursor to the Musama Disco Christo Church, it was reported that angels held a crown over the head of Catechist Appiah when he was fasting, indicating that he was destined to become a great king. Hannah Barnes, his wife-to-be, saw in a vision seven angels ordering her to climb the ladder that they had brought down from heaven. They also gave her a Bible with the command to go on an evangelizing mission with Catechist Appiah.

When the early followers were expelled from the Methodist Church in Ogwan and later when they were persecuted by others for their beliefs, the Angel *Gabriel* exhorted them to remain faithful. God also sent a special angel, *Jehu*, to respond to the requests of the Faith Society. Later in the Church's history, encounters with angels also became a regular part of the experience of leaders and members within the Musama Disco Christo Church.

To enable his followers to understand something of his spiritual experiences, Prophet Amoaforo frequently described what was beyond the perception of most human beings through use of analogy or metaphor, describing the unknown in terms of the known. Only those who have had such experiences can fully appreciate his efforts to articulate them in human language. These descriptions were not intended to be taken literally, but they gave people a way to put in words the reality they represented. Some were spiritual, others were intellectual, or were metaphors drawn from human experience.

The Prophet also had other kinds of spiritual experiences, ones that he described as traveling to the astral realm. "Astral travel," "heavenly ascent" or "spiritual journeys," were also themes in the Bible and in other religious traditions as well. Essentially they constituted the ability to transcend the limits of sensory experience and materiality through the development of an expanded consciousness. For Prophet Amoaforo and his followers they were spiritual gifts.

The angels once showed him a prayer cloth with a design on it of three red circles broken in two sections, a blue circle with four blue wings tipped in red radiating from it, and then three yellow circles broken into four segments. The colour red symbolized the blood of Jesus; blue was for victory and gold for wealth. The Prophet and others who sat on the cloth reciting specific psalms for seven days and keeping candles burning in the room would be carried away to the astral world.

At other times, Prophet Amoaforo said that when he would go into his room, lie on his bed and tell himself that he wanted to go to a certain place, the power would take him there. Sometimes he traveled with his body; at other times his body remained in place while his soul ascended. He did not necessarily name a specific place that he wished to visit when he traveled spiritually.

Prophet Amoaforo was also transported by various metaphorical spiritual jet-like planes. The planes were identified by name: Hibroma, Hirosia with seven wings, Smaila, Diayama, Kamara, Siyama. One of the Taliva planes was one hundred miles in length and traveled at a rate of 335 miles per second. He also traveled on two planes called the double Taliva and the fourth Taliva. On one planet, the Prophet also rode on white horses with silver headgear.

The Angels and Mehu

Among his space travels on earth, Prophet Amoaforo traveled to India to meet with several important spiritual leaders there. He also traveled to New York to find an Asante soccer player when his family lost contact with him, and to Kumasi to assist his brother's wife who was ill. He planned to make trips to Australia and Italy in the future, though he did not live long enough to undertake them.

When Prophet Amoaforo talked about angels, he did not describe their appearance, though the wall paintings at Mehu employed the usual metaphorical iconography of winged beings clothed with white robes. He described the astral realm as a universe with stars, moons and suns.

Prophet Amoaforo's remarkable relationship with the angels began during his tailoring days at Koforidua and continued throughout his life. His first awareness of encountering angels came after the curing of Madam Addo, the tailor's wife. The angel *Helasalisa* and the great angel *Halbasak* compelled him to complete a ninety-day fast during which he learned about the mission he had been given in life. After his conversion to the Musama Disco Christo Church, Jemisimiham Jehu-Appiah, Akaboha I, gave Prophet Amoaforo the heavenly name, Jenasman, meaning "master of the angels who produce thunder," shortly after the outset of his ministry for the Musama Disco Christo Church, further expressing his close relationship with the angels.

Although angels appear to have guided Prophet Amoaforo's early missionary activities, it was in relationship to Mehu that Prophet Amoaforo's encounters with angels reached their fullest expression. He learned that the people who came for healing suffered both spiritual and physical ills that were caused by Satan, who was considered to be a fallen angel. So he waged a continuous struggle with Satan during his ministry. Prophet Amoaforo was guided and protected in this ministry by the constant presence of good angels.

One Sunday, sometime around 1984-85, the angels reminded Prophet Amoaforo of his mission to establish the "Great Nation," Mehu, at Senchi in order to help people with their daily needs, and to save mankind spiritually. In preparation for the founding of the earthly Mehu, Prophet Amoaforo fasted for two years and seven months from pepper, meat and salt, and bathed at midnight so he would not be seen.

During the fast he undertook to establish Mehu, Prophet Amoaforo first visited Heaven, which was located below the Heavenly Mehu and above the planets. Some of the angels lived there as did a group of "divine sages" or "enlightened masters" who had attained spiritual perfection and did not need to return to the earth. Humans can go to heaven, the Prophet said, but those not sufficiently developed spiritually will be required to return to earth to continue the process of purification.

Then Prophet Amoaforo was taken up in a chariot driven by mighty heavenly horses past Heaven to view another Bigger Nation beyond Heaven named Mehu. He described Mehu as "a hanging nation held by golden chains studded with glittering diamonds". It was not stationary but moved between the heavenly realms. As it descended, thunder and lightning ignited and then the *Cherubim* and *Seraphim*, a Band of seven Angels each, fell down in adoration to the Lord and shouted: "Holy, Holy, Holy, Lord God of Sabbath, Thy Glory has filled the heavens, earth and beneath the earth." According to Prophet Amoaforo, the distance between Heaven and that Heavenly Bigger Nation, Mehu, was 4,000 miles. This Mehu was sealed all round with gold and was about 1000 miles in circumference. It was inhabited by special Mighty Heavenly Beings called *Jahuus*.

On that first visit to the Heavenly Mehu, Prophet Amoaforo felt that something was inserted inside him that functioned like a video camera. Later, when he was back on earth and wanted to review what he saw there, he switched on the machine to play back the scenes. Once again, this must have been his metaphorical way of speaking about spiritual visions that he had been given.

When Prophet Amoaforo visited Mehu for the second time, he observed that "the gold encircling it was sparkling like a welder's fire, so he could not go near it again. He asked the angels who took him there why this was so. They replied that when he was first sent there, the fire was subdued to enable him to draw nearer to behold it. Since the second visit he did not go there again."

Perhaps the language Prophet Amoaforo used to describe these two trips to Mehu was influenced literally by the biblical descriptions of spiritual journeys made by the Prophet Exekiel in his Throne

The Angels and Mehu

Chariot vision in *Ezekiel* 1. Prophet Amoaforo's chariot was driven by mighty horses similar to the chariot with four wheels that took Ezekiel up to the heavenly throne. The language of Prophet Amoaforo's description of the Heavenly Mehu is also reminiscent of Revelation 1. Both of these Prophets attempted to describe the divine being they encountered as well as the heavenly realm itself, but Prophet Amoaforo did not try to do so, probably because among the Akan the divine being is not represented visually.

During his astral travels which extended throughout his lifetime, Prophet Amoaforo visited a number of planets, 555 in all at his last count, shortly before he died. Each of the planets had a distinctive form, structure or design, and each had its own distinctive celestial or heavenly inhabitants, forces or powers. During his astral travels, the Prophet visited a number of planetary mountains, which, he said, were populated by distinct beings. He described some beings on these planets as ones that did not need light, water, money or food, nor did they reproduce.

The pre-existent *Narseeners*, who lived on the Kandara Mountains, the seat of God, had large dimensions: heads of 12 feet, a breadth of 30 feet, a height of 300 feet, ears of 3 feet, hands of 4 feet, and legs of 6 feet. He reported that these planetary mountains had bases of 500 miles in circumference and were 5,000 miles in height. It was at the Kandara Mountains, the Prophet believed, that Moses received the Ten Commandments, a variant on the account in the Hebrew Scriptures.

The *Adras* beings, similar to the *Narseeners* in size, lived on the 335th and 334th planets respectively. They acted as Deputies of God, while the *Jahuus* served as His ministers. The *Narsineers* and the *Adras* sat in conclave or as a parliament, receiving, examining, and answering petitions from suffering humanity, sent to God through the *Jahuus*. According to the Prophet, the *Jahuus* were higher than the angels. They were clothed in white apparel and lived in perfect holiness. The angel in charge of all the planets was *Delelu*. Other angels there included *Bimajaja*, *Kilmajaja*, *Jaja-Majaja* and *Jaja-Ojaja*.

Other planets, in the form of mountains, included: Mandara Mountains, the source of energy for the Earth's sun, moon and stars; Omandara Mountains, the source of rainfall that controlled the earth's vegetation; the Famandara Mountains, the source of air or wind for the earth planet.

Kimakaro, the 21st planet, was a star planet or the abode of stars, carrying 77 special stars of the universe, where *Nuhu*, the high angel of that planet, traveled at a speed of 3,500 miles per second through the other planets. The source of wealth was located on Kimakaro, controlled by the angel *Habu* and his associate angels, whose main functions were to distribute wealth to devotees, and to solve the financial problems of petitioners.

Prophet Amoaforo encountered the star called Dominita with its distinctive musical beat on the Makatapi, in the astral realm. The Prophet was given a small stone in the shape of a star that later became part of a monument in the Akwamu area erected by Prophet Amoaforo so that people in the region might prosper.

Prophet Amoaforo claimed that the angels on Skandara Mountain mined metals or produced equipment for the spiritual armies. On Heemajakasi Mountain the blacksmith angels manufactured aircraft, steamships and all types of weapons for the *Hajaja* angels. Along with the *Hajaja* army led by the bullet-proof *Donora*, Michael and his team fought *Lucifer* for three hundred years before *Lucifer* was defeated.

The *Sikapanos* Angels manufactured war weapons for the Garo Army, who were heavy artillery fighters led by the Angel *Ziriiyo*. They lived on Pimagaro Mountain, and, together with the *Hajaja* Army led by *Donora* and *Michael* and his team, then fought *Lucifer* for 300 years before the latter was defeated.

Omaharo was the Mountain of Darkness. The *Sikatinas* Angels, with *Garasi* as their leader, inhabited this mountain. They joined *Donora*, *Michael* and their teams of angels to defeat *Lucifer*.

The 15th planet called Osa was known for its good vegetation. That was why the Prophet, who was from the planet Osa, also provided his family and those who visited Mehu with food and fish from his gardens and fish ponds. The Prophet was told that there was a spiritual pillar called Vonopoli on the 15th planet. He said that "it has a sweet element in it so anyone who visits it goes back with that sweetness in his/her life".

In addition, Prophet Amoaforo visited planets under the sea and their angelic and earthly human inhabitants. Some of these beings, he said, do not die, as humans and sea creatures do. Among them, the *Fomabus* angels formed a special security army located 8,000 miles beneath the Earth planet. The *Tuners* angels were the blacksmith angels who live 4,000 miles beneath the Earth Planet. They were about one foot in height and were vegetarians. They manufactured weapons and aircraft for the *Fomabus* angels. At 2,000 miles down lived the *Bramabus* who were immortal. The Prophet also received a revelation in 1992 about the *Holiers*, angels who existed before creation and were located about 25,000 miles below the sea.

Whenever a whale came ashore to die, the Prophet explained, it signified, symbolically, the presence of human life in the oceans. That event occurred to inform us, the Prophet said, that some great human lives had been lost deep in the ocean world. There were angels, too, in the rivers, trees and forests and rocks, the Prophet asserted, but he claimed not to know much about them.

Prophet Amoaforo was able to travel spiritually on earth as well as in the astral realm. In one instance, when he returned to Koforidua at the request of the Akwamuhene, Nana Kwafo Akoto, Jenasman saw a vision of himself flying in the skies in a vehicle with sparks of light falling from it like hurricane fire. He heard someone shouting and calling the names of several towns as he passed by them – Accra, Weija, Winneba, Keta, Denu, Aflao, Lome, Benin, Ouagadougou, Kumasi and so on. Suddenly the vehicle bumped into a house.

Jenasman landed on his feet in Kumasi where one of his brothers lived with his wife. He found the wife very sick and almost dying. He said he was being transferred to Senchi in the Eastern Region and promised to send his brother a telegram the next day so he could bring his wife for treatment. As soon as the brother read the telegram, his wife got up and felt better. He later brought her to Jenasman at Mehu and she was eventually healed. She also gave birth to a child there.

After Prophet Amoaforo's fast and travels to the Heavenly Mehu in the late nineteen-eighties, he proceeded with the construction of the Mehu Healing and Retreat Centre at Senchi Ferry in the Eastern Region of Ghana. The complexity of the astral realm and the profuse number of angelic and other spiritual beings that Prophet Amoaforo experienced there is reflected in the equally complex structures, symbols and other unusual representations found at Mehu.

Prophet Amoaforo claimed that the word Mehu came from the Musama heavenly language (*osor kasa*), meaning "located in the land of Egypt". He considered Egypt to be synonymous with Africa, referring to Isaiah 19:19, "In that day shall there be an altar to the Lord in the middle of the land of Egypt, and a pillar at the border thereof to the Lord." In ancient literature, Africa was referred to as Ethiopia. Although the biblical passage described the structure as an altar, the Prophet maintained that Mehu was not an altar, but a Great Nation, symbolizing God's Glory and Power on Earth. He cited Psalm 68:31, "Let Ethiopia hasten to stretch out its hands to God," as justification for God's establishment of Mehu in Africa.

Some Musama people voiced their objections to locating Mehu at Senchi. They thought it should be built in some more prestigious area of the country, such as Mozano. But Prophet Amoaforo indicated he had been directed specifically to build Mehu at Senchi. The shrine was dedicated upon its completion by Prophet Miritaiah Jonah Jehu-Appiah, Akaboha III and General Head of the Musama Disco Christo Church on June 28, 1987.

Prophet Amoaforo welcomed the angels sent to Mehu to assist him in carrying out healing rituals, delivering prophecies to the community, and teaching those who visited Mehu how to live so as to become spiritually developed persons. In this way, Prophet Amoaforo and Mehu at Senchi together created a bridge between the spiritual and the earthly worlds that enabled humanity to realize its full divinely ordained destiny.

The word Mehu was used by Prophet Amoaforo in several different ways. God had revealed to him that the Heavenly Mehu was "a Great Nation," embodying Church, healing, chieftaincy, traditional religion, Islam and everything on earth." It was difficult for most people to grasp the nature of Mehu, due to the fact that Prophet Amoaforo used the term Mehu for several different realities.

First, Mehu was the universe above Heaven where God and the people who had become fully developed spiritually lived after death, together with other high angels. It was, as the angels called it, a Great Nation, the full body of those who are spiritually developed, who have been allowed to return from earth to the heavenly realm without being sent back.

Mehu was also the name of the healing centers that Prophet Amoaforo set up during his missionary work for the Musama Disco Christo Church, the last and most important of which was located at Senchi in the Eastern Region of Ghana. The Prophet insisted that Mehu was radically different from a Church, even Musama, because it was not simply an altar or a shrine or a healing centre. Mehu at Senchi, in the Prophet's view, was a place for worship, spiritual development and meditation, a place of healing to which countless people came for salvation and deliverance from all the ills that affected them. The Healing Centre aspect of Mehu was simply one way that the Prophet sought to fulfill the purpose of the spiritual Mehu.

The first monument the Prophet built at Mehu was also called the Mehu. It is made up of three short concrete circular wall enclosures. It was intended to have seven walls and circles, according to the design given to the Prophet by the angels, but the funds were not forthcoming to complete the design. However, there are four enclosures built outside the main body of the monument, two to the left and two to the right.

In constructing Mehu, Prophet Amoaforo considered it part of his mission to recreate visually the images he saw of the Heavenly Mehu. He also drew inspiration from the designs he had been given by the angels while he worked as a tailor at Koforidua. At that time, the angels instructed him to record a number of symbols that the Prophet then painted on cloth. He was told they would play an important role later in the construction of the earthly Mehu at Senchi. These symbols, Prophet Amoaforo stated, were the beginning of Mehu.

Central to the physical design of Mehu were three hearths, one of which burned all the time. The angel *Jehu* was sent to work with Prophet Amoaforo at Mehu, as that angel had also been commissioned to assist the young Musama Disco Christo Church. He was assisted in his mission by other angels, called *Jahuus*, who were under his direction. In addition, the *Gashi* angels kept watch at the hearths to protect Mehu, in accordance with Psalm 121:4 which stated that "the protector of Israel never dozes nor sleeps."

The Mehu, the first structure of the complex built by Prophet Amoaforo, has a rectangular entrance. Seven stars at each side of the main entrance of the Mehu represent the *Cherubim* and *Seraphim*. There are also three stars on the pillars in the gateway to each side of it. The one set of three stars represents the three wise men and the other set Mary Magdalene and the other women who visited the tomb of Jesus. On top of the entrance is a representation of Jesus, the war captain. A red anchor hangs in the gateway and indicates that the Lord had established it. The key emphasizes the same metaphor: "I the Lord am the Key; when I open nobody closes; when I close nobody opens. I am *Kiki Tara Bee*", meaning "key" in the heavenly language of the Musama Disco Christo Church.

To the left of the main entrance, there are six stars on the walls of the front outer enclosure and six on the walls of the back outer enclosure. The stars represent the twelve apostles. There are also three steps at the doorway of these two enclosures. Like the three steps in front of the main entrance, these signify the Trinity. The angel in charge of the gate here is *Nathani*. This structure acts as a parliament building for the *Jahuus*.

The other gate has seven stars representing the *Cherubim* and *Seraphim* and the seven virtues, namely, charity, joy, peace, patience, benignity, mildness and endurance. The five stars represent the five letters in the name of Jesus. The large star at the arched top of the gate is called the Dominita, meaning dominion of God. The Makatapi monument at Akwamufie is also topped with the Dominita star.

On the other side of the façade, there is a great crest that carries the likenesses of the three Akabohas, Prophet Jemisimiham Jehu-Appiah, Akaboha I, Prophet Matapoly Moses Jehu-Appiah, Akaboha II, and Prophet Miritaiah Jonah Jehu-Appiah, Akaboha III, and the first Akatitibi, Prophetess Nathalomoa Jehu-Appiah. A red anchor hangs on the outer gate of the Mehu that the devotees pass under to exit. The angel *Hatimo* is in charge of this outer gate.

There is a circular space made by the three concentric half-circular enclosures at the center of Mehu on each side of the gate. The largest and the outermost concentric half-circular walls have forty-eight representations of stars. The middle one has fourteen stars each and the innermost ones each have seven stars. The stars again represent the *Cherubim* and *Seraphim*.

The central part of the Mehu has three white crosses, one larger and higher than the two in front of it, towards the outer gate. The larger cross represented the cross of Jesus and the others are those of the criminals with whom he was crucified. The chief angel here, the chief of all the *Jahuus*, is named *Jalago*. The Cross, Spiro, is said to represent the ignominious death of Jesus for our sins. This is the supreme sacrificial symbol and the cornerstone of faith in Jesus as Saviour.

This section of the Mehu is where individuals, both Musama Disco Christo Church members and non-members, come to make their private petitions. They expect to receive prompt answers and the *Jahuus* oblige by dealing, usually successfully, with their requests. The angel *Habu is* responsible for the offerings made here. He is thought to multiply the offerings that are made to God by petitioners seeking an answer to their prayers.

Two sets of wells flank the two gates of the Mehu. The wells and the water in them on the right side of the main gate are consecrated for the healing of mental patients, epileptic patients, cases of tuberculosis, evil spirits and witchcraft, burning sensations, bodily pains, rheumatism and the like. These are considered spiritual diseases. The two wells to the left are for the healing of the childless, pregnant, blind, dumb, lame and other clients. There is also a set of wells at the outer gate of the Mehu, one on each side of the gate. The water from these wells is used for the spiritual baths prescribed by Prophet Amoaforo in healing rituals.

A special chamber called the Simahu, the fertility centre, is built along the right side of the Mehu for women seeking pregnancy and safe delivery. It is triangular in shape with walls just as high as those of the Mehu. Water from the well is used to heal them in this enclosure. On an inside wall of the Simahu, a blue cross is inscribed inside a red circle. The same design appears in red on the outer wall and in other areas in Mehu.

Outside the main structure there are enclosures called the Saras that are the prayer areas. They are intended as the place for sick children to receive healing. The Mehu is considered spiritually too hot for children. There are again three steps at the main entrance where the *Majaja* and the *Omajaja* angels protect the healing activities conducted there.

The Simahuta is a structure at Mehu that has walls with twenty-four stars on them. At the apex of the outermost wall there is a white cross. The middle one has a round yellow pillar with a seven-pointed star on top of it. There are also five stars on the pillar itself. The innermost is a pillar with a gold crown on top of it. At the foot of the pillar there is an inner sealed chamber with three stars on each side. This inner chamber was intended to house a special monument and a stool that was intended to be shown seven times, with seven gunshots and the sounding of the trumpet seven times, indicating that Mehu was entering a new year. This project was not completed at Mehu before the Prophet's death, however.

The Sala-Mehu is both the spiritual armory for the Mehu and the place for the confession of sins. It is shaped almost like a trapezoid. The walls are up to the height of an average man. The gate of this monument has red representations of the sun, moon, and stars on top. The wall painting there depicts Jesus wearing a crown of thorns. Below that on both sides are five stones, representations of the missiles of David (I Samuel 17:40). A red anchor hangs in the doorway. It symbolically locks the sins of the devotee entering the monument to confess his sins and to ask for the forgiveness of sins under a cross in the monument. The inside is empty except for a large cross.

The *Ajaja* angels inhabit the Sala-Mehu. *Donora* is their leader. Symbols on the outside of the building include the head of John the Baptist signifying spiritual bravery unto death, and a corpse and skeleton symbolizing humility unto death for the warrior Christian (I Timothy. 6:6-8). There is also an axe for the strong power of the Musama Disco Christo Church. The ladles, kettle, cup and utensils represented there depict the various items used in performing "systems" or rituals that take place at the Sala-Mehu. Different types of "Taliva planes" that are used for wars in the astral realm are also depicted on this monument.

Other representations on the outer walls of the Sala-Mehu include the double-edged sword, Ayemidi-Kusidi, symbol of the first Akaboha and Akatitibi of the Musama Disco Christo Church, a truncheon, bow and arrow, spears, ship and a bulldozer. There are also representations of the red cap and slippers of Prophet Amoaforo, and the all-seeing eye and the all-hearing ear of God. A pair of scissors and a blade represent a shaved head and a body of cleanliness.

Crossed British and French flags representing Europeans are also painted on several walls at Mehu. In one place, the crossed flags are accompanied by a portrait of Akaboha I, Jemisimiham Jehu-Appiah, representing Africans. Portraits of powerful religious leaders such as Gandhi, Sri Prabhupada, Mohammed and Krishna and his Mother symbolize the spirit of inclusivity that Prophet Amoaforo cultivated at Mehu.

The Prophet constructed the Victory Stone in May, 1990 to signify the victory of Jesus over death. The Victory Stone is five sided, symbolizing the five letters in the name of Jesus. Prayers and offerings are made here for devotees to be as victorious in life and over death as Jesus was.

Between 1987 and 1989, Prophet Amoaforo constructed another monument, the Nuhu/Kimakaro, controlled by the Heavenly Mehu. This is a replica of a monument on the 21st planet. It is a twelve-sided star of prosperity that moves through the 335 planets at a speed of 3,500 miles per second. The angel *Habu* is in charge on this planet.

Prophet Amoaforo built the Helobim, a big star, in the year 2000. A monument to the *Helalalaahu* shepherds and also one showing a hand raised, and the inscription, "Africa has lifted her hand," were erected next. Construction continued at Mehu up to the time of Prophet Amoaforo' death, with the final structure, the Prophet's tomb, built afterwards.

When Prophet Amoaforo constructed Mehu, he always had angelic protection there. In 1986, he prophesied that *Jimahaji*, "a beautiful and glorious angel" had been delegated to stay there permanently. The angel *Nathani* is the gateman of the main Mehu entrance and *Hatimo* is the angel in charge of the outer gate. *Jehu* and the *Jahuus*, God's cabinet ministers in Mehu, control the Sun, Moon, Stars, Wind, the Earth planet and the whole universe. They use stones as missiles. Their leader is *Jilago*, the controller-general.

The Kimakaro is controlled by the angel *Habu*, whose linguist is the angel *Hadra*. *Habu* is the spiritual controller and source of wealth. He is in the middle of the three crosses within the innermost circle of Mehu, and always doubles any offering given at Mehu. *Hascona* is secretary in Mehu, and *Hiro* is the leader of the *Sandras* angels who provide babies to women who come to Simahu, the Mehu Fertility Centre.

In addition to the angels associated with specific shrines at Mehu, there are battalions of warrior angels there. The *Hajaja* angels including *Ajaja, Hajaja, Bimajaja, Omajaja, Zimajaja, Sajaja* and *Ojaja-Ojaja*, use spears, bows and arrows and other weapons to fight the principalities and powers of darkness. They use spiritual "Taliva airplanes" of great power and versatility. The *Ajaja* angels drive out of the Sala Mehu anyone possessed by spirits from any river or mountain or from within the bowels of the earth.

The angels *Zimagaro, Gimagaro, Magaro-Magaro, Omagaro-Magaro, Bimagaro-Magaro, Samagaro-Magaro, Garo-Garo* and their leader, *Ziriyo*, are special angels that fire heavy spiritual "guns" in the Heavens. The angels *Gashi, Bimagashi, Omagashi, Zimagashi*, and *Gashi-Gashi* are special "tear gas angels" who protect God's people from evil forces with cosmic sacred fire. *Simacus* is the angel who guards the Simahuta. The *Yamadutes* are the angels who punish souls after death.

In addition to these more or less permanent resident angels at Mehu, other angels who were sent on special assignment to serve at Mehu were revealed periodically to Prophet Amoaforo.

On April 28, 1985, the angel *Jimahudu Abima* was sent to supervise the work at the Mehu and fight the demonic forces to glorify God. The prayer for the system was: *Jima Ala, Buma, Akuni, Sapa Bama Mashey Elohim Jahahu, Napakama Aduna, Jidima. Amen.* This is an untranslated prayer in the heavenly language.

God, through prophecy to Prophet Amoaforo, confirmed that the formal opening of Mehu would be held on Sunday, the 10th of November, 1985, instead of the date announced earlier, October 6, 1985, but promised that the Angels would descend on the original date to help prepare the grounds for the opening.

On January 1, 1989 the Holy Spirit promised to send the angel *Hunahuna* to draw close to the people in their individual lives, and on December 18, 1989, Jenasman was informed that the ruling angels for 1990 would be the *Hunkaros*, among the greatest angels in the higher realms. Their utterances were final and conclusive; they were not deceptive; they did not go back on their word. These angels, that came from a place in the heavenly realm where the wind was strongest, were to account for all happenings on the earth planet and to supervise all powerful manifestations that would occur during 1990.

The *Zimarias* were sent to help serve from January until June, 1990. They were to perform many miracles that would be beyond human understanding. At the same time, the *Malakos* angels, who used *Halaga* spears that had fiery ends and the power of lightning, were sent to protect the yard at the Mehu. They were warriors who fought fiercely behind the *Hajaja* army.

On March 3, 1990 it was revealed to Prophet Amoaforo that the *Hamakamos* angels would bring down a wind to the earth planet with which God would stir himself during 1990. And on April 4, 1990, the Prophet was told that the angels called *Hamis* were delegated to follow the seven angels who would move from east to west from Good Friday, April 12 to Sunday, April 15, 1990. They would return to their destination on January 1, 1991.

The *Hamis* angels were followed by the *Bimakus* that would form a big knot in the atmosphere, causing shaking and trembling in the universe throughout the rest of the year. The ruling angel for 1991 was to be the angel *Handra*, a mighty angel on a level with the *Jahuus*. In 1991 the people of Mehu were advised to invoke the *Gowers* angels to mellow the calamities that would come up that year.

The ruling angel for 1992, *Simagus*, was revealed to the Prophet on December 22, 1991. He was told that *Simagus*, a Senior Angel, would start his journey from south to north, bringing a tough time for mankind. The *Sanarious* angels, who held a very strong fiery wind with clouds, would move with the ruling *Simagus* angels to handle mankind in 1992. And on December 25, 1991, the Prophet learned that the *Hangros* angels would be sent down from January until June, 1992 to minimize the troubles that would befall mankind from January, 1992 onwards. Also, the angel *Saban* would descend to stir the sea violently in 1992, thus causing difficulties in fishing and creating shipwrecks and the sinking of boats.

On December 6, 1992, the Prophet was informed that *Haidro*, "the Bomber," would be the ruling angel for 1993. He and his team of angels, who had red fire around their heads like a turban, would be in charge of this earth planet from 1993 until 1999. Their mission was to judge the activities of all angels in the higher realms. They had a pair of scissors called "Bitawa" which they used to cut the money bags of financial agents, causing the exposure of every transaction.

On June 28, 1993 Prophet Amoaforo announced that a special angel, *O.U.*, would be the power that would lead the community in the second half of the year. At the end of 1994, he revealed that the angel delegated to be in charge of the yard was named *Pilatano*. This angel was described as "mighty, swift and fervent." *Pilatano* did not allow people to do what they liked in the yard. He performed many wonders, the sick were healed, the barren brought forth, the poor were assisted and petitions were granted.

At the end of 1994, Prophet Amoaforo revealed that the angel *Dredger*, "a big grinding machine," would be the ruling angel for 1995. This angel caused the heavens and the earth to shake vigorously, creating an unstable situation for humankind. The Prophet also identified a group of satanic angels, called *Hamblers*, who came to tempt evangelists to perform miracles after preaching. Many were disgraced if they could not perform miracles.

The prophecy that Prophet Amoaforo received toward the end of June, 1995 indicated that the angel *Mahuduhu* would lead Mehu in the ninth year, 1996. At the end of July in 1995, the Holy Spirit promised to send the angel *Sugar* from the sugar planet, with the result that everyone coming to Mehu would experience sugar-sweetness in their lives. The Holy Spirit also promised that many angels would be released to work at Mehu that year to draw people from all parts of the world. These angels would bring wealth, children and other valuables to them.

The angel *Shapner*, accompanied by a multitude of angels, was prophesied to be the ruling angel for 1996, which was predicted to be a difficult year with many deaths, poverty and other calamities. The name *Shapner* means "Razor." The Prophet said that if the people did not follow God's wishes, they would be trimmed by the razor of *Shapner*.

In the second half of 1996, the Ruling Angel was *Goodily*, signaling an era of goodness and truthfulness. God also sent angels, led by the angel *Handorious*, who bring heavy rain storms and thunder. They were responsible for destroying buildings and for airplane crashes, among other disasters, but also for releasing an adequate supply of fish into the waters.

God revealed to Prophet Amoaforo on December 28th, 1996 that the ruling angel for 1997 was *Rockner*, meaning "rock of ages," and that 1997 would be another difficult year. God also promised to send angels called *Checkers* whose job it was to check on everyone's activity. *Adra* angels were also promised for this year. They carried a large pair of scissors to expose private corruption to public view, and demanded strict and total accountability of everyone. In the second half of 1997, *Hintarago* was the ruling angel designated to monitor the perfection and righteousness of mankind.

Prophet Amoaforo announced on June 30, 2002 that the angels serving at Mehu for the coming five years would be the *Roma*. He also revealed that he would go to the planet Kaskatara for six months to help stranded souls before his departure from this life.

On the morning of June 9, 2003, Prophet Amoaforo stated that the angel S*hiomaama* had been delegated to take charge of the 16th anniversary celebration at Mehu. "His shining glory is like the morning sun. He has come to change the mourning of the afflicted into laughter. He has come to reveal a lot of things and everybody will be happy in life." Prophet Amoaforo also added: "Musama is a good Church; it is capable of doing everything through God's power from now on. Mighty Beings have fallen because of Mehu. God is victorious."

On August 24, 2003, Prophet Amoaforo reported that a number of angels from the 14th planet had been sent to Mehu. The leader of these angels was *Maripauma*. The responsibilities of these angels were to unveil God's purpose for Mehu and to show forth the glory of the Musama Disco Christo Church; to display the glory of Africa to the whole world for God's glory; to reveal God's love for Africans; to support Ghana.

On Christmas day, 2004, Prophet Amoaforo revealed that the angels sent to fight on behalf of the Musama Disco Christo Church crisis were *Sedra* from the 44th planet and *Onaana from* the 55th planet. He said they will work from east and west at the beginning of the year to finish the work at the Musama Disco Christo Church by the middle of the year.

On January 1, 2005 Prophet Amoaforo said that God had sent two angels with a special "komo" gun to intercede on behalf of the earth dwellers. This gun had 27 outlets.

The presence of angels at Mehu, which the Prophet numbered in the millions, and also the spiritual soldiers there, gave Prophet Jenasman Kwadwo Amoaforo the confidence to work without ceasing to bring about the mission for which Mehu was created: to restore Africa to its former status; to liberate people that Satan had chained; to enable the barren to have children; to comfort the afflicted; to heal the sick; to feed the hungry; to clothe the naked; to help the poor/unemployed; to produce books that will aid in the spiritual development of the soul. A review of his work at Mehu as well as during his missionary activities demonstrates how effectively Prophet Amoaforo fulfilled the roles to which he was called.

The success of Mehu and of Prophet Amoaforo's work there was confirmed by a message that the Prophet delivered on the 15th anniversary of Mehu, June 30, 2002: "God has wonderfully performed miracles since the establishment of Mehu in 1987. God delegated special angels to work here for the first five years. They performed their duties diligently, excellently. A different set of angels was sent to Mehu every five-year period since then".

Toward the end of his life, Prophet Amoaforo said: "I pray God to give me strength to continue and accomplish the work he sent me to do and take me away when I am due to leave this earth planet. Mehu is going to stir the whole world for both the Black and White to know that power belongs to God who is capable of doing all things. My mission is to assist the whole world. I thank God and all of you who helped in diverse ways to help in the accomplishment of Mehu. May God bless all of you."

On June 30, 2006 Prophet Jenasman Kwadwo Amoaforo, Senior Superintendent Prophet of the Musama Disco Christo Church completed the mission that God had given him. He died and was buried at the Mehu Healing and Retreat Centre at Senchi in the Eastern Region of Ghana in September of 2006.

Before his death, Prophet Amoaforo prophesied that his successor

The Angels and Mehu

would not arrive for fifty years, and that the chosen prophet would come from India. It will be a long wait before a gifted person such at Prophet Amoaforo comes again into the world to manifest the attributes of an avatar, revealing the qualities of the divine in the human world for the benefit of mankind.

Chapter Three

Healing and Ritual

The angels guided and prepared Kwadwo Amoaforo for his spiritual mission unerringly throughout his early years until he encountered Musama Disco Christo Church missionaries at a healing ceremony in Koforidua, where he had been apprenticed to a tailor named Mr. Addo. Then an extraordinary event occurred that would become one of the major turning points in his life. It began like this.

One day, Mr. Addo asked Kwadwo to accompany him and his wife, Kwakyewa who, after two years, was not able to get pregnant, to the place where the Musama Church people were preaching. When the preachers prayed and touched Mrs. Addo, they began to shiver. Then Kwadwo picked Mrs. Addo up and he began to shiver himself. This was his first experience of faith healing, but he thought it was the work of local deities.

Kwadwo came back and reported his experiences to his fellow apprentices. He said he felt very uncomfortable after that experience and would not go to the Musama Church people again. However, Mr. Addo shamed Kwadwo into visiting the preachers once more, hoping he would witness something different. Reluctantly, Kwadwo agreed. As he approached the Musama people, Kwadwo reported that he felt something holding on to his legs and shaking them.

Suddenly he found himself in the midst of the preachers. He began to push them away from his master's wife. He drew her to his bosom and started shaking, chanting some incantations and prayers. After some time, he calmed down and sat. He had apparently healed Kwakyewa of her barrenness. However, he still attributed his healing ability to the work of a local divinity and regretted going back there.

Apparently, among the ways in which human intuition can express itself, one is medical intuition, the ability to perceive the bodily energy or lack of it emanating from a human body. This perception allows the intuitive to identify possible sources of disease or torment in the patient and then to do healing work on them. Before this incident, Prophet Amoaforo was not aware that he had this gift, but that he did was demonstrated many times thereafter in his healing work.

Everyone present marveled and the preachers themselves thought it was a miracle. They said, "Even we who brought the religion from Fanteland have not yet experienced such a thing." Kwadwo, still puzzled at what had happened, replied that he didn't know what happened; they would have to decide for themselves. He left and returned to his master's workshop. Then he tried to drink off the matter, purchasing a half penny's worth of palm wine. Since drinking was against the doctrines of the Musama Disco Christo Church, Kwadwo thought he could avoid the spirit that had possessed him by drinking.

Shortly after that event, however, Kwadwo encountered two angels, *Helasaliza* and *Halbasak*, during a fast he undertook. Following the fast, he ended up becoming a convert to the Musama religion. The angels also took him under the water for several days to further prepare him for his mission. These events were only the beginning of the exceptional experiences he would have throughout his lifetime.

Undoubtedly inspired by the angels who watched over Kwadwo, the missionaries brought stories about Kwadwo Amoaforo to the attention of Jemisimiham Jehu-Appiah, Akaboha I, Head of the Musama Disco Christo Church. Guided by inspiration, Jemisimiham Jehu-Appiah realized that Kwadwo Amoaforo was the one destined to complete the building of the Church and welcomed him warmly. The Akaboha gave him the spiritual name Jenasman, meaning "master of the angels who produce thunder". In 1943, the Head Prophet also installed him as a Junior Prophet in the Musama Disco Christo Church.

The angels could not have directed Kwadwo more appropriately, since the spiritual gifts that Kwadwo received were perfectly in accord with the mission of the Musama Disco Christo Church, to heal the sick and to overcome the destructive demons in the universe. The Church, an independent Christian Church under African leadership, already had developed a powerful healing tradition when Kwadwo Amoaforo first encountered the missionaries and the Akaboha I.

Following the fast and his commissioning as a Junior Prophet of the Musama Disco Christo Church, Jenasman traveled around the Gold Coast preaching and healing. He reported that he cured hundreds of people of barrenness, madness, bodily burns, fits and spiritual diseases while on his missionary journeys.

Later, in the Akwamu area Jenasman encountered another local priest of Tigare. This was the main local divinity worshipped in the Akwamu area. It tormented its followers and killed almost ten people a day under all sorts of guises. One day Jenasman told his pastor he thought they should go and save the people of Akwamu, especially since they were distantly related to him through his mother. The priest was said to have seized all the jewelry, gold and other precious ornaments of most of the people in this area as an appeasement to Tigare who had accused them of being demons.

When they arrived, Jenasman approached the priest of Tigare who had threatened to kill him. When the priest asked him why he had come, Kwadwo said he had been informed that the priest was holding many of his people captive and he was there to deliver them and their property. The priest replied, "Young man, do you want to go back to Koforidua alive or dead?" Jenasman asked him what he meant, and they exchanged comments. As the exchange went on, members of Jenasman's family pleaded with him to give up his encounter with the priest and his efforts to redeem his people. But he persisted in his demand to collect all the confiscated property from the priest.

The priest of Tigare got up angrily and dashed towards his room shaking as furiously as fire. He decided to bring the stolen goods to Jenasman since the priest thought he was evil. Jenasman asked the people to take the goods but they would not do so because they feared the repercussions. They said that he should carry his 'luggage.' himself since they had not demanded anything from Tigare. Jenasman carried off the gold and jewelry while more than 500 people booed him.

Jenasman then warned the priest Awuah, and his wife, Odaamea, that he would capture and conquer them, and by 8:00 a.m. the next morning they would experience something terrible. One of them would die. When Jenasman returned to his uncle Dampare's home, the man was frightened and told Jenasman to flee at dawn. But Jenas-

Healing and Ritual

man assured his uncle he would conquer the priest and his wife. That night he had a spiritual encounter during which he went into space and met the couple, who had also transcended into space. When he saw them, Jenasman dashed at them and attacked them. He struck the wife of the priest with the machete he had in his hand and she fell prostrate.

Early the next morning, as the priest started the daily rituals, the atmosphere suddenly became solemn. The priest's wife was lying down prostrate, almost dead. Jenasman's uncle could not believe the prophecy of the night before had been fulfilled, and he wanted Jenasman to escape from potential danger. Jenasman reassured him as a large crowd following the priest came to the uncle's door. The priest pleaded with Jenasman to release his wife from bondage. Jenasman asked the priest to go and wash the woman clean and send her to her father's house where Jenasman would meet her.

When Jenasman and his entourage arrived, they prayed intently and Jenasman had a spectacular vision. He saw a spirit moving in human form out of the dead woman. He rushed upon the spirit and grabbed it firmly, and together both of them fell on the dead woman. As they fell, she opened her eyes and exclaimed, "I am alive." Everyone was amazed and thought that Jenasman was a wizard. Thereafter, the woman became a convert to the Musama faith, as did others in the crowd.

On another of his missionary trips, Jenasman was accused of holding the local Tigare in contempt. He was summoned to the house of the Chief, Nana Kwafo Akoto, who laid the charges before him. The plaintiffs were 25 powerful priests of Tigare who maintained that he had abused or insulted Tigare. As the Chief presented the charges, Jenasman asked who exactly the 'person' of Tigare was, since no one there called himself Tigare. They said Tigare was the deity they worshipped. Jenasman then challenged Tigare to punish and kill him. The Chief duly dismissed the case, leaving it to the deity to respond, and told Jenasman he could go and hope that he would be alive in the morning. Tigare did not respond and Jenasman lived and continued his mission.

Prophet Amoaforo followed the tradition of the Musama Church that grounded its healing activities first on the belief in God as the healer and also on the life and work of Jesus the healer. The founder of the Church, Prophet Jemisimiham Jehu-Appiah, who was expelled from the Methodist Church largely because of his practice of faith healing, emphasized that Jesus commanded his disciples to cure in his name and not with medicine, so they should do the same.

The Musama Disco Christo Church as well as many other indigenous Christian Churches also drew upon the practices of traditional Akan religion that integrated religion with healing. Like them, Musama concerned itself with all dimensions of life, not just the spiritual aspect. When Jenasman became one of the designated healers in the Musama Church, he set up mission stations in areas such as Koforidua, Nsawam and Swedru and also established more permanent healing camps, which he called 'little Mehus' in these places.

The procedure that the Musama Disco Christo Church followed for a patient seeking healing at Mozano and the healing camps included the following steps that Prophet Amoaforo generally observed at Mehu as well:

1. The patient would come to the camp with a relative or supporter (*Kyigyinafo*) This person was expected to stay with the patient throughout the healing process. The healer would inform the *Kyigyinafo* about the cause of the ailment and tell him or her there would be no charge for healing, following the practice that Prophet Jemisimiham Jehu-Appiah had been instructed by God to observe. However, the *Kyigyinafo* was expected to make an intercessory offering and promise a votive offering at the successful conclusion of the treatment.

2. The healer would then begin a period of fasting and prayers for guidance about how to proceed with the healing. The healer might also learn about the causes of the patient's problem. If the cause was considered to be possession by an evil spirit, the patient would have to want to have the spirit exorcised before healing could take place.

3. A ceremony was held to mark a successful healing after the patient had informed the healer of his/her recovery and the healer had prayed to God for the healed person's protection. The patient then fasted for three days which ended when the healer laid hands on the person. The *Kyigyinafo* was then informed about the successful

outcome and a date was fixed for the *asubo* ceremony when the healed person would be presented ritually to the community, and relatives would join with him/her to thank God for this gift and to pray for strength, protection and purity.

The donation (*anohoba*) promised by the *Kyigyinafo* made at the beginning of the healing process was then offered. It should be noted that generous gifts and donations, including four cars, were given to the Prophet by those who benefited from his healing work.

The Prophet followed the older practice in the Musama Disco Christo Church in not using drugs for healing. He usually employed only natural elements, such as water, stones, sand, palm fronds, candles, Florida water, *Kazatu* (a mixture of izal, brimstone and several other ingredients), fire and oil in his healing systems.

Prophet Amoaforo recognized that water had spiritual power. Water appeared at the beginning of God's creation and it was used by Jesus in his healing work. Water was also recognized as having intrinsic power to sustain human life. In fact, without water humans could not continue to exist. So the Prophet always used water in his healing systems.

Prophet Amoaforo was also directed in the use of water for healing by Mr. Lamptey whom he met while living at Nsawam. Mr. Lamptey predicted that the Prophet would always live near rivers, so that the powers in the rivers would help him in times of crisis.

At all his healing shrines, the Prophet required clients to take a holy bath as both a necessary prelude to ritual, and as a means of dispelling evil spirits. It was also carried out on a private level daily or weekly by devotees striving to live a sanctified life, to keep the spirit clean, to subdue evil forces, and to heal and open greater possibilities for people.

The water in one of the wells at the Mehu, known as Himara water, is used for holy baths. The bathing preparation also contained Florida water and stones. When it was used for expelling demons, izal and brimstone were added. The Prophet said that, because of the prayers offered regularly at Mehu, the angels came to charge the water and make it effective. A patient who bathed with it and drank it would be healed.

The holy drinking water, Tamara, is located in two wells at

the outer gate of the Mehu. The two wells to the right side of the main gate were consecrated for the healing of mental and epileptic illnesses, tuberculosis, evil spirits, witchcraft, burning sensations, and bodily pains, such as rheumatism, all of which were classified as spiritual diseases. The two wells to the left were for the healing of patients who were blind, dumb and lame. A special chamber, the Simahu, near the wells was used for women seeking pregnancy and safe delivery. Outside the main structure, wells called the Saras were used for sick children to receive healing with water.

A detailed report of Prophet Amoaforo's healing work with a particular woman over an extended period provides a significant insight into the Prophet's healing work using water.

In 1962, while working at the Koforidua Court as a member of the clerical staff, this woman became ill and consulted a doctor. After a second occurrence, she was admitted to St. Joseph's Hospital at Afidwaase Koforidua for further observation. After three weeks, her Aunt, Afua Difie, her mother's sister, told the woman she had asked the doctor to release her so the Aunt could take her for healing to Prophet L. K. Appiah at the Musama Church in Koforidua. Pastor Forson from Mozano was also involved.

The treatment began with baths of *kazatu*, during which she was allowed to wear only her panties. This preparation was thought to be good for driving away evil spirits. She was also required to drink holy water about five times a day and at midnight. She had to stay at the mission house in Koforidua with her aunt for intensive treatment.

When her condition improved, the woman was massaged with oil specially prepared for healing rituals. This process happened about three times a day. The patient was allowed to wear some clothes during these rituals. The woman's mother provided the patient and her Aunt with food while they were at Koforidua.

After a week, the woman felt better and had a dream in which someone told her to remove the pajamas that she wore in the hospital. When she did, the person put the clothes on a corpse. The following Sunday at Church, one of the Church elders spoke under inspiration to tell her to thank God she was alive. He said if she had stayed four weeks in the hospital, she would have died.

When Prophet L. K. Appiah felt that he had reached the limit of his capacity to help this woman, he asked her mother for permission to send the woman to Prophet Amoaforo. She agreed, and the group arrived at Senchi and met Prophet Amoaforo who asked for their mission. Then he sprinkled the client with Florida water and told them that the devils in her family wanted to change her destiny (*nkrabea*) from a bright future to the opposite. He said he would have to perform a system for her at midnight to avert the situation. The system was performed that night and the following day they returned to Koforidua.

The client returned to Senchi periodically over the next five years, because she suffered recurrences of her problems. The Prophet said that some diseases took longer to heal than others. Prophet Amoaforo advised her to join the Musama Church because the mainline Churches, like the Presbyterian Church to which she belonged, could not deal with cases like this. She accepted this advice and became a staunch Musama member.

The first time she attended a Peace Festival at Mozano, the woman asked God about the source of her problems. The answer came to her in a dream that night. She saw two women from another branch of her family, a mother and a daughter, standing by quietly while she sang and wept. She learned that these two women were the source of her problems. Later, she was told about the two houses of the Abooso Royals and their rivalry in the family for the stool. Apparently one result of the devilish activities of these two women was that she, the patient, was not able to have children.

Around 1989 or 1990, this client got severe stomach ulcers when she took some drugs by mistake. She returned to consult with Prophet Amoaforo and again was healed. Finally she undertook to work with the Prophet at Mehu, keeping records at the shrine and organizing its activities.

Thanks largely to her efforts, systematic records were kept about the healing and other activities of Prophet Amoaforo at Mehu. These records followed the patterns established at Mozano. The various types of physical illnesses of people brought to the shrine were documented, with details of the person's name, date of arrival, the type of problem, the Musama Church Station from which they came, when they were baptized, the relative who brought them, the outcome of their treatment, and the amount of their contribution to Mehu.

The Prophet generally followed the systems set up for healing at Mozano, adapting them according to the inspiration he was given by the angels. Prophet Amoaforo, like the early Musama Church healers, did not use medicines of any kind, but simply relied on natural elements and trust in God. He, like they, used specific approaches to healing different diseases.

The healing of madness, which was considered a spiritual ailment, usually took place at midnight and involved special prayers. Cases of barrenness required douching while drinking holy water. Dumbness and lameness, which were considered to be caused either by demonic forces or as a result of evil done by the patient, required repentance by the patient. If these conditions were considered to be the result of sin committed by relatives, prayers for forgiveness were said, and both the healer and the patient fasted.

Examples from the Mehu records include the story of a mad man who was abandoned by his family and stayed at Mehu for more than a year undergoing treatment. Finally, Prophet Amoaforo went to the astral realm and pleaded for him to be healed. The angel *Makarios* at once responded to the Prophet's petition and healed the man. Early the next day, the man saw the Prophet and told him he had been healed. The Prophet pretended he did not know about it and asked him, "Is it true?" and the man responded "Yes". He continued to live at Mehu and helped at the shrine for a time and then returned to his family. Then some time later he returned to tell the Prophet he had gotten a job and that his family now accepted him.

A woman trader from Akosombo who reported she had a misunderstanding with someone over money and had been cursed with *juju*, also came to Prophet Amoaforo for healing. She complained that her neck ached terribly and it affected her whole body. After two weeks of treatment at the shrine, she was healed.

An army officer came to the shrine reporting that he had a severe and persistent headache. Earlier, he had obtained protection from another shrine in the form of a snake put on his head. As a result of this treatment, he had heaviness, aches and burns on his head that were terribly painful. Once his head was shaved and healing was

Healing and Ritual

done on him for over a year, he left the shrine. He later recovered and became a full member of the Musama Disco Christo Church.

Once, the Prophet performed a system for a woman in Kumasi who was not able to have a child. After she had the baby, she refused to honor her pledge and as a result her second child died. When she went to another shrine to consult about her deceased child, she was told that she should go and fulfill her promise to the Prophet who first assisted her. So she came to pay her vow of 25,000 Cedis and to show her first child, a girl, to the Prophet.

A madman from Anum who had been healed promised to return and pay his vow of four thousand Cedis, but he didn't do so. After three or four years, he arrived back in chains. When he consulted the Prophet, the Prophet asked him if he and his family had paid their vow. They replied negatively, so the Prophet advised them to go and pay, which the family did, and immediately the man was healed. Then the Prophet ordered his chains to be removed by the Pastor in charge.

The Prophet also assisted people with their material needs. For example, a woman consulted the Prophet about finding capital for a business. After she took the holy bath, someone offered her money as capital. She showed the Prophet the money before she began her business. Another person who needed money came to the Prophet and afterwards won 1.2 million Cedis in a raffle.

The Prophet recognized that some families had evil forces associated with them. When they died, these evil forces remained. If someone inherited from them and used their possessions, such as clothes, the force would be transferred to them. If they were fortunate enough to meet a master like Prophet Amoaforo, that person could assist them to get rid of these evil forces.

According to K. Ampom-Darkwa, who studied the records of the people who visited Mehu between 1987 and 1998, Prophet Amoaforo's clients at Mehu could be classified into four categories: individuals who were sick with spiritual diseases, and required admission to the Camp as inpatients; people with various life problems for which they sought help as outpatients; people seeking spiritual development to reach a higher plane in the spirit world in the fulfillment of their destiny and those seeking messages of national and international import.

562 persons were recorded as having come to Mehu as inpatients for assistance during this period. The four leading complaints reported by the patients whose cases were recorded included unspecified spiritual diseases (191), body pains (63), mental problems (54) and pregnancy issues (57). Ninety-nine of every hundred cases brought to the shrine were successfully resolved, and people traveled from far and wide to consult the Prophet. His ability to cure an average of four inpatients a month was an outstanding record, according to Darkwa.

Prophet Amoaforo frequently used his encounters with angels and travels to the astral realm to assist him in healing his clients. He also summoned angels to come to Mehu to help him with certain cases, such as with the request of an Asante royal family to find their son in New York, or he transported ill persons to the astral realm for healing by the angels.

The Prophet reported that he had power to fight demons. He said there are some people who can see and say a lot of things about a person but cannot go to the battle field to fight on a person's behalf. This special gift that he had gave him the confidence to take on local priests and divinities as well as the evil spirits that harassed people.

Metaphorically, Prophet Amoaforo said, the bad spirit in people is like an engine, so the Prophet would at times call someone to sit by him for a chat and joke with him. During that time he dismantled the engine so that by the time the person left the Prophet's presence, the engine was not functioning. At other times, the Prophet told witches and wizards to go for the normal systems stipulated to cure other sick people, or he directed them to go individually and pray by the hearth.

Prophet Amoaforo kept a collection of "magical" objects that were surrendered to him by people who had possessed certain demonic powers. A woman gave him a cloth that could turn her into a cobra (*onanka*). A pipe once belonged to a woman who smoked it as she flew to conduct her sinister operations. The smoke was said to protect her. A certain cloth item could carry a woman away when put on her hand. Another, worn around the waist, could help a person vanish. A talisman, when put around a person's neck, enabled a person to come into someone's room at night to destroy them. A cloth with cowries sewn upon it was said to turn into a snake or fire when worn. A whisk used for devilish operations and activities was also included in the Prophet's collection.

Prophet Amoaforo also kept an object from his own encounter with demons, the skeleton of a dead bird. The Prophet reported that one night after he began the construction of Mehu, he heard an unusual noise in his room where the door was locked. The demons, in the form of a bird, had come to fight him. The Prophet says he picked up a big stick with which he killed the bird.

The owners of these 'magical' items told the Prophet that, after they were healed, the devilish spirits sometimes came back to try to control them again. So the items had to be returned to the Prophet to have their powers destroyed.

In addition to the healing activities and personal consultations carried out at Mehu, rituals were conducted regularly, some on a daily basis, others at agreed intervals. Among the most powerful were those involving the use of fire. Biblical examples were used as precedents for the use of fire in rituals at Mehu, including Exodus 3:1-6 that recounts how God appeared to Moses as an inconsumable flame of fire in a bush and announced that He was the God of Abraham, the God of Isaac, and the God of Jacob (3:6).

Additionally, the time of Pentecost also provided a model for the use of fire. The Holy Spirit appeared in the form of tongues of fire and settled on the people after Jesus' death and they were given spiritual gifts such as speaking in tongues. The Prophet also described God as a consuming fire, whose heat ripened the righteous but consumed the unrighteous (Matt 13:24-30), so that the dross would burn away.

When the congregation assembled and encircled the fire during rituals at Mehu, they did so with the faith that God would use the fire to purify and sanctify them and make them clean and holy in His sight. Through the fire, it was believed, God would burn away all their spiritual and physical problems, whether self-inflicted or caused by others.

Prayers were said around the three hearths at Mehu morning, noon and evening. Prophet Amoaforo reported that because he moved with fire, he always bought firewood to keep the fire burning.

The Prophet, Jenasman Kwadwo Amoaforo, in a pensive mood.

ABOVE: *The Prophet J. K. Amoaforo as a child, at age six, with his parents.*

BELOW: *The founder of the Musama Disco Christo Church, the Prophet Jemisimiham Jehu-Appiah, and his wife, the Prophetess Natholomoa Jehu-Appiah.*

ABOVE: *A painting at Mehu depicting Adam and Eve in the Garden of Eden, where beasts and humans lived in harmony before the Fall of man.*

BELOW: *The great star, Helobim, on the 95th planet and the great key of the planets, called Huhuuma.*

ABOVE: *A hand in the mist of stars, signifying God's plan for the restoration of Africa.*

BELOW: *The Kimakaro, a star of prosperity on the 21st planet.*

A shepherd angel on the 25th planet.

The Akaboha III, Head of the Musama Disco Christo Church.

The victory stone signifying the victory of Jesus after the Resurrection.

The Makatapi at Akwamufie, symbol of prosperity and blessing for the people of Akwamu.

ABOVE: *Simahu, the fertility centre at Mehu.*

BELOW: *Members of the research team interviewing the prophet.*

ABOVE: *Prayers around one of the three hearths at Mehu.*

BELOW: *The congregation, with paim fronds and lighted candles, lined up in front of Mehu during the 10th anniversary celebration.*

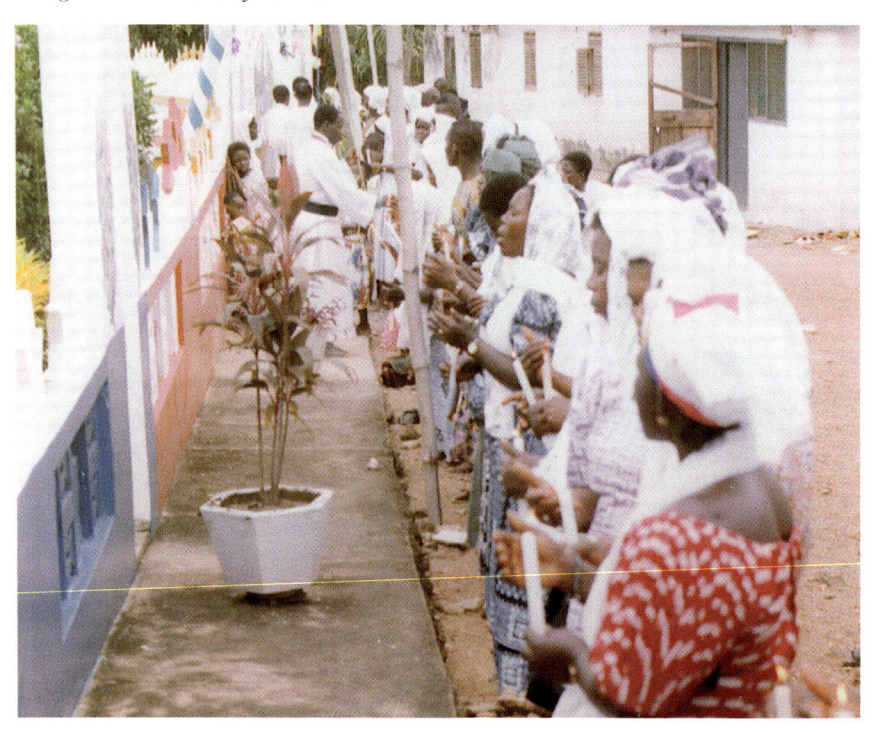

x

ABOVE: *The prophet on his 82nd birthday with some members of the congregation.*

BELOW: *Healing at Mehu.*

The Prophet with the sheep from the Church headquarters as a vindication of the 1979 prophecy.

The ever-burning hearth was near the Prophet's consultation area. This was the hearth where the *Gashi* angels, the special angels who controlled the power of fire, resided.

The Prophet reported that when he used the fire hearths and prayed for a patient, the *Gashi* angels carried his prayers up to Heaven for priority treatment. Alternatively, the Prophet might take the patient up to Heaven to be worked on by an angel, or an angel would come down to Mehu to do the healing. This latter healing activity was in fact the mode that Prophet Amoaforo used when a member of the Hare Krishna community in his area was sent to Mehu suffering from madness and asked for healing.

The Prophet stated, "Where there is fire I am always there. I am always by the hearth praying because God is fire, and I never fail. Fire gives light and life, sight and sound. Our hair is fire and does not rot at death. There is also fire on our toes. Fire is life."

The Prophet said he went into the center of the fire spiritually to charge himself to fight spiritual battles. It was said that when the Prophet charged himself like that, you could not defeat him because he was from fire and water. Nor could the devils go near fire.

A second fire was located near the Huma cross, a site for rituals, where the *Spiro* angels resided. The Huma cross was said to represent the ignominious death of Jesus for human sins and was considered a redemptive symbol. A third fire burned near the road close to the entrance to Mehu.

Prayers were said by the Pastors at the Mehu three times a day throughout the year: morning, noon and evening. Three lighted candles and three palm fronds, *merekensono*, were used in the mornings and evenings, but not at noon. The number of candles might be increased, depending on the number of people available. In the mornings, between 5:30 and 6:00 a.m., before going through the Mehu, the conductor of the service rang a bell seven times to call the team to enter the Mehu. The conductor stood facing the entrance.

When the team members (four in 1998) had taken their positions in the Mehu and lighted the candles, they held three candles and three palm fronds. The conductor did not hold a candle or a palm frond, however. He rang the bell seven times. The team faced west in the mornings.

Candles were used in this and many other Mehu rituals because they were symbols of light and illumination as well as a manifestation of the sacred. Palm fronds were also used because, as vertical forms, they expressed a link between the human and the spiritual realms, much as both Prophet Amoaforo and Mehu also represented this link for devotees. Palm fronds are also symbols of joy, victory over one's enemies, over the flesh and the world.

At the morning ritual, the conductor stood in the front, while the rest of the team stood behind him and prayed aloud alone on seven different topics. After that, all prayed together on the same seven topics with intermittent songs between prayers. The Lord's Prayer followed, and afterwards, the team, with the exception of the conductor, took positions in the Mehu, either to the left or to the right, as they chose. The team members all raised their hands and prayed for spiritual strength. When the conductor observed that the individual prayers were over, he rang the bell once and the prayer session ended. Then the assembled group left the Mehu through the entrance.

At noon, the pattern was the same, but no candles or palm fronds were used. This time the team faced east, standing at the outer gate during the prayers. In the evening, the pattern was similar to that at noon, but candles and palm fronds again were used. The group faced east, standing at the outer gate. At the end of each session the group departed through the main entrance. Any time candles were used during prayer services, they were extinguished at the end of the prayer session. The palm fronds were left in the Mehu to be used later.

Prayers were also offered in the Kimakaro for the first seven days of each month. At the entrance to the Kimakaro, seven candles were lighted and put on the ground. The position of the pastors was the same as it was in the Mehu. The bell was rung seven times. The conductor prayed three times. Then the team also prayed three times, with intermittent songs. The Lord's Prayer was said, and the ritual ended. The team departed from the Kimakaro after the Lord's Prayer.

Prayers were offered at the Huma or Big Cross twice a day throughout the year, in the mornings and evenings. The conductor did not hold a candle, unless he was alone. In that case, he lighted three candles and put them on the ground. As many as seven or eight people might attend the ritual. The bell was rung seven times. Prayers were offered as at the Mehu, seven times on seven different topics. The prayer session ended with the Lord's Prayer. The team then left the Huma.

Every morning after praying at the hearth, the pregnant and barren women assembled in front of a cross in the centre of the yard to pray at the cross near the Huma shrine where the *Spiro* angels resided. After praying they marched toward the Simahu, the fertility centre, singing. The pastor in charge led the women in prayer here again, and they drank a cup of water specially consecrated for the purpose, given to them by the conductor. They then returned prayerfully to the cross where they began and then dispersed. After the prayer, the gongon was sounded or rung three times before the group left the Simahu. This ritual was carried out two times a day, morning and afternoon around 4:00 p.m. throughout the year.

At the time of the Annual Festival at Mehu, as well as on other occasions, Prophet Amoaforo distributed blessed stones and small portions of sand to devotees. He referred to stones as "missles of the Jahu angels", and he explained that the use of stones in the Musama Church went back to the time of the first Akatitibi who used to give small stones to members.

The stones had the power both to protect devotees and to enrich them as well. However, most people, because of their low level of development, did not understand the spiritual power of stones. The angels, on the other hand, used stones because there was power in them. The Prophet said that if people had blessed stones in their houses, the angels would draw near to protect them.

The stones distributed by the Prophet usually came from the sea where they washed up along the Labadi-Teshie Road. He fasted and performed systems on them to consecrate them before he distributed them. Sometimes he recharged the stones of individuals when he noticed that their power was low.

The Prophet said that recipients had to use their stones regularly by praying with them as the ritual instructed, that is, every morning and when in distress. When he collected and squeezed a stone, he

Healing and Ritual

was able to tell if it was powerful or not. If it was used regularly, he could feel some heat in it; otherwise it would become cold.

Prophet Amoaforo also distributed sand to devotees, primarily to the fishermen for a good catch, and sometimes to traders to help them attract customers. When the sand was sprinkled on the nets, it blindfolded the fish and they were attracted into the net without becoming spoiled. After the Prophet had collected the sand from the beach, he fasted and performed some systems on it to make it powerful, just as he did with the stones.

The Prophet said that sand had power. He observed that when God made the sea, which moved continuously with its waves, God also made sand to stop the waves from moving further. He recognized, however, that the sand underfoot also had the power to work *juju* on people.

Each year, the establishment of Mehu at the Senchi Healing and Retreat Centre continued to be celebrated on or near June 28 of each year. The celebration lasted from Thursday to Sunday on the dates announced by the Prophet and the officials of the Centre. The following is a description of the Anniversary Celebration that was held in 1997.

On Thursday the Reverend Ministers in the district arrived at Senchi. In the evening around 7:00 p.m. the formal opening was done with prayers. The Resident Minister led the group first to the Mehu, then on to the Spiro Cross where the angels dwelt. This was the place where the community assembled each morning, afternoon and evening to present their petitions and pray to God. The petitions included prayers for the sick at the camp; members with individual problems; and family and national problems. The ceremony continued with songs, including *Yewo Nyame a ohwe yen daa* ("We have a God who provides or cares for us daily"). A short sermon was then given and the ritual closed about 9:30 p.m. A sacrificial bonfire was made to give thanks to God.

As the group prayed, they held palm fronds which they used to sprinkle themselves with holy water after prayers. The palm fronds were then thrown into the fire to burn. This was done when people presented prayers at times of greatest need. From there, they went to meet as a congregation to celebrate the tenth anniversary of the founding of Mehu.

On Friday, there was communal labour on the road leading to the yard and general cleaning in the house to welcome more visitors. Regular Mehu rituals were also observed.

On Saturday, the 28th of June, the anniversary celebration began with a bonfire. The Prophet Elisha, after fasting, prayed to God to let fire destroy the works of Baal and take his sacrificial offering. So also the congregation performed this ritual to burn away the acts of the evil forces and to accept the sacrifices of the Prophet and his followers to signify the victory of his followers.

Rituals then continued according to the normal practice described above. Prayers continued at the Mehu and at the Huma Cross where the *Spiro* angels resided. The Cross was viewed as a redemptive symbol for the community which regarded the Cross as a supreme sacrificial symbol and acknowledged it as the cornerstone of their faith in Jesus. Healing and fasting continued during the day, with a break called between 11:30 a.m. and noon. An opportunity was also provided for individuals to consult with Prophet Amoaforo.

In the evening, prayers resumed at 7:30 p.m. and ended with a bonfire between 11:30 p.m. and midnight. The sick, the spiritual prisoners, the weak and those burdened with sin were invited to encircle the fire for sanctification. The songs sung on this occasion were *"Ogya no mmera, ommera mmehyew bone nyinaa"* ("Let the fire descend to burn all evil.") and *"Yewo Nyame a ohwe yen daa"* ("We have a God who provides or cares for us daily").

Sunday's activity was the climax of the celebration. Those who had not come earlier started to arrive. There were people from Accra, Kumasi, Koforidua, Mozano and the Asuogyaman District. A representative of the District Secretary, usually the Assemblyman of Senchi, and a minister deputized by the Akoboha III were also present. Choristers came from Akosombo and Atimpoku. Their songs included *"Onyankopon, aman nyinaa beyi w'aye, aman nyinaa beda w'ase"* ("God, all nations will praise you, all nations will thank you") and *"Nyame Ye"* ("God is good").

Awards were presented to the Prophet, the Assistant Prophet who helped the Prophet found Mehu, and Professor Kofi Asare Opoku who was appointed Nkosoohene of Mehu. After being enstooled traditionally, the Nkosoohene swore an oath of allegiance to Mehu and he addressed the community to acknowledge the honor. The Prophet then addressed the assembly.

After prayers by the congregation and an address by the Tema Minister on "Pulling down the Stronghold of Satan" there was a sacrificial offering by the Minister-in-Charge of Akosombo. The congregation offered monetary sacrifice while the Choristers sung *"Eye a mensuro, ene Nyame nam a, eye a mensuro koraa"* ("Do not be afraid, if you walk with God, be not afraid"). The fire was encircled again to offer sacrifices through prayers and thanksgiving, while the choristers sang, *Yewo Nyame a ohwe yen daa* ("We have a God who provides or cares for us daily").

The congregation then adjourned to the Mehu where the Senior Minister and a female assistant welcomed them. Members were anointed with oil on their foreheads while the person being anointed held a candle and a palm frond. Then the members went through the Mehu. The ceremony concluded about mid-afternoon so that people who had come from a distance could return home.

Radio coverage of the programme was provided by the Volta FM station. It included the District Secretary's speech as well as that of Prophet Amoaforo, concluding with a song by the choristers.

Prophet Amoaforo fulfilled his designated mission as Healer in the Musama Disco Christo Church over a long lifetime. He healed diseases, protected and delivered people from the destructive forces of the devil and other demonic spirits, wherever they resided. He fed the hungry and clothed the naked, and helped the unemployed. But there were additional aspects to his mission that have not yet been examined: his prophetic revelations and his commitment to preach the true gospel of the unity of all religions, all races and nations with a common destiny. It is important also to examine these other ways in which Prophet Amoaforo laboured throughout his life to carry out his mission and his divinely appointed destiny (*nkrabea*).

Chapter four

Prophecy

Prophet Jenasman Amoaforo was blessed throughout his life with remarkable intuitive spiritual gifts of prophecy as well as the healing powers that were discussed in chapter III. He, like Prophets of other times and places to whom these gifts had been given, often experienced them as a heavy burden, but one he and they agreed to bear. His gift of prophecy was acknowledged and respected in the Musama Disco Christo Church community that had a strong prophetic tradition as well.

Once, when Prophet Amoaforo was asked how he got the prophecies, he said, "I ring the angels." Asked what number he rang, he said, "I use a password, just as Ali Baba and the forty thieves used 'Open Sesame.'" Though humorous, the Prophet insisted he did have a direct way of communicating with the angels and receiving prophetic messages.

In more serious moments, the Prophet indicated that he received revelations during his heavenly ascents. He once explained that he and the angels communicated in a kind of "Morse Code" set of dots. When he returned, he reported to his assistants at Mehu that he had received a prophecy or revelation. He then translated the "Morse Code" communications into his language. Each assistant separately translated them into English. They compared their versions of the prophecy and, together with Prophet Amoaforo, established the official version which was then distributed widely.

There was apparently no systematic record kept of Prophet Amoaforo's prophecies prior to 1980, with the exception of the 1950 prophecies about the building of a spiritual monument and a dam in the Akwamu area. These prophecies were recorded in the volume, *The Prophetic Ministry of Jenasman K. Amoaforo*, published by Rev. S. K. Jehu-Appiah in 1987. The work was sponsored by the Akaboha III, Miritaiah Jonah Jehu-Appiah and was an assignment from the Musama Disco Christo Church Literature Committee to commemorate the official dedication of the Senchi Healing and Retreat Centre on Sunday, June 28, 1987. The work was revised by the Mehu Committee in 1994.

Another set of Prophet Amoaforo's prophecies began to be collected some years later by Pastor M. K. Agyei. These prophecies were compiled by M. Naiandrina Streetor with the collaboration of M. K. Agyei, M.L.K. Jehu-Appiah, K. Buckman, the Mehu Committee Members and others. They were published under the title *Prophecies* in 1997. Later prophecies have been preserved at Mehu but not published. The earliest prophecy in this collection is dated to 1980 and was delivered to the Adjenahene, Nana Twum Barima and his elders about the future of their town in the Eastern Region of Ghana.

Three different categories of prophecies are identifiable. The first type includes the prophecies made over a number of years about the development of the Akwamu area. A second category concerns Mehu and includes the annual prophecies intended to prepare people for the challenges of the coming year. The third category, historic as well as historical in nature, addresses the corruption in some of the leadership of the Musama Disco Christo Church and focuses on its leader Akaboha III, Miritaiah Jonah Jehu-Appiah.

All three of these categories contain prophecies on certain themes and extend over a period of time. The first group concerns the material as well as spiritual welfare of the social community in the Akwamu area. The prophecies on Mehu in the second category are God-given guidance for Prophet Amoaforo on how he was to construct Mehu as a bridge between the spiritual and the created worlds and the rituals to be used there to further Mehu's bridge-building mission. They also give guidance to people on the issues they confront in life and how to respond to them spiritually. The third category is intended to avert a major crisis in the Musama Disco Christo Church and to return the Church to its spiritual foundations and practices.

Early in his missionary work, Prophet Amoaforo had a vision that he was going to receive some special spiritual power to help build Africa. So when he received a prophetic message for the Akwamuhene, he lost no time. He visited Akwamu Mangoase and told the elders that he had a message for the Akwamuhene. Then, accompanied by Messrs. Otchere Debra and E.C. Appiah, he crossed the Volta River by canoe and arrived at Akwamufie. When he met the Akwamuhene, Nana Kwafo Akoto, the Prophet told him that he had been directed spiritually to build a monument in Akwamu.

The Akwamuhene finally agreed to accept this prophecy, and in 1947 Jenasman, with the consent of the Akwamus, had a monument called Makatapi built at Akwamufie, a location established by divination, according to the suggestion of the Akwamuhene, Nana Kwafo Akoto.

The monument was constructed in the following way, according to the Prophet: "Every citizen of Akwamu collected stones, prayed on them for their wishes, and brought them for the foundation. Seven Holy Bibles were encased in the foundation. The monument was constructed of seven circular levels. Each level had one of the seven Bibles in it, and a biblical text was inscribed on the stone (Gen 31:46). The structure was crowned by the Dominita star and had many smaller stars on it as well. Prophet Amoaforo predicted that the Makatapi would be a source of blessings for all in Akwamu for seven years. Then the blessing was renewed for another seven years as seven more Bibles were added to the structure.

Prophet Amoaforo further prophesied that the Makatapi would make Akwamu an "Eye of God" in the Gold Coast and it would bring many jobs to the area. Additionally, the Gold Coast would win its independence from Britain; and the new nation would be led by the Dominita star. The Makatapi was dedicated in 1951 by Akaboha II, Matapoly Moses Jehu-Appiah.

Meanwhile, surveys and reports were already being drawn up in the late 1940's and the 1950's for the construction of a dam along the Volta River in the Akwamu area. So, with the spiritual guidance of the Dominita, and with the consent of the Akwamuhene, the Prophet traversed the Akwamu forests and showed them the area that would prosper.

The Prophet indicated with small white flags where roads would be constructed. He marked a place near the Volta River and said to Nana Kwafo Akoto, "In this place a bridge will be built over the river in the near future, and lorries and cars will travel to Akwamu." Nana and the people who heard the prophecy said they were worried that the Musama religion was making Jenasman crazy.

The construction of the Adome Bridge was of great significance for the Akwamu area. Previously the only means of traffic to the Akwamu area was across the Volta River by ferry boat, a dangerous option. Some boat owners pirated the passengers or deliberately threw their passengers into the river in order to take their cargo. With the construction of the bridge, however, roads became an important facilitator of regional commerce.

Jenasman also predicted that white people would come to the Akwamu area, and that a modernized society would emerge, symbolized by men and women wearing the same kinds of trousers and coats. In fact, colonial explorers, intent on tapping into the area's natural resources, had come to survey this area by the beginning of the twentieth century. A South African surveyor named Duncan Rose had plans drawn up for a dam on the Volta River by 1940 and then came to survey the area in order to make plans for the dam's siting. He did not say exactly where the dam would be built, but it is said that Jenasman was directed spiritually to the exact spot and pointed it out to the people.

Jenasman also prophesied that Atimpoku, a village in this area along the Volta River, would become a bustling commercial township where schools, a hospital and other amenities would be developed. This was one of several towns in the area that hoped to be chosen as the site of development associated with the dam project.

The Volta Dam construction project began in 1962 and by 1965 the Akosombo Hydroelectric Project, constructed by an Italian company, was completed by the Ghanaian government with loans from the World Bank, the United States and Britain. The Volta Dam, in addition to supplying power for aluminium production, also generated electricity for the Gold Coast and a few neighboring countries. The Volta Lake transport also came into operation at this time; various commercial facilities were established, including Akosombo Textiles Limited at Akosombo and Juapong Textiles

Company; a banana farm also began production and export.

Prophet Amoaforo's interest did not stop with the construction of the dam and businesses in the Akwamu area, however. The township of Adjena in the Akwamu area had also been considered as a site for the hydroelectric plant that ultimately was built at Akosombo. Because Adjena was not chosen, the economic and social development of that town was seriously curtailed. But on December 25, 1980, Prophet Amoaforo was sent to Nana Twum Barima, the Adjenahene, and his elders and townspeople to predict an improvement in their situation in the near future.

Prophet Amoaforo told Nana and the people prophetically that the blessings God had bestowed upon them earlier had improved their lot, but then Satan began to fight against them, building a wall around the town. But because of the people's prayers, God demolished the wall and enabled them to move to a higher spiritual level. A flag was also raised on a high hill to indicate that victory had been won. Angels were to be sent to Adjena to assist the people.

This prophecy assured the people of Adjena that their time for prosperity had come. They were told that that they should stay in unity and love, and do all things in common. If they did, then progress would come to them. He said that within five years Adjena would have electricity, fine streets, and the town would expand. Foreigners would come to buy land for a large market; a government hospital and a police station would also be provided for the town. The angel *Hero* ("quick helper") would be sent to assist them. Finally, a stone was erected to assure the people of God's blessings to come.

During the period of the Akwamu prophecies, Prophet Amoaforo carried out his ministry in Akwamu and at Senchi, where he had set up a healing camp and retreat centre in the mid 1960's. It was similar to the "little Mehus" that Prophet Amoaforo had set up earlier in other areas.

Prophet Amoaforo's healing camp at Senchi was the direct predecessor to the Mchu Healing and Retreat Centre that he established on the site in 1987. He undertook a special fast lasting two years and seven months beginning in 1984 during which he received further revelations about Mehu and the work God wanted him to do there.

Prophecy

The 1997 collection, *Prophecies*, included prophecies directly related to Mehu and to the yearly prophecies that Prophet Amoaforo delivered after the formal establishment of Mehu as one of the official healing camps of the Musama Disco Christo Church.

On Sunday, August 18, 1985, the Prophet delivered this prophecy: "I, God, am still moving within you. Do you remember I told you I will start to demonstrate my power? I have started. I will perform many miracles beyond your reason and it is not from any man, but Me, the Creator; so start to wash your clothes white as snow in order to be able to draw near to Me, the Lord. Regarding the sick, barren, pregnant, and diverse petitions, we shall not turn back, but will move ahead. I will continue to guard your families, wives, children, relatives, so that there will be peace in your family circles."

On Sunday, July 20, 1986, the Prophet delivered a powerful prophecy about Mehu. In it, he was identified thus: "Jenasman is a Warrior from heaven sent down to support Nana Miritaiah Jonah Jehu-Appiah, Akaboha III and General Head Prophet of the Musama Disco Christo Church." This prophecy probably reflected the reconciliation that took place between the Akaboha III and Prophet Amoaforo a year earlier.

The prophecy describes Mehu as a "beautiful nation" that will be a showpiece and will attract people from East and West. It will consolidate the African continent spiritually and physically to the glory of God. It will possess power, strength, wisdom and knowledge. It will demonstrate its power to both blacks and whites. Whatever in the past that could not be performed or achieved, will be accomplished through Mehu's thunder power to the glory of God.

Connstruction of the main shrines at Mehu continued for two years. In spite of the reconciliation between the Akaboka III and the Prophet, the Musama Church did not provide any direct financial support for the project, since some Church leaders wished to see first what would come of it all. Contributions from clients and friends provided the necessary resources. Mehu was officially dedicated on June 28, 1987 by the Akaboha III and General Head of the Musama Disco Christo Church, Miritaiah Jonah Jehu-Appiah.

In a prophecy given on December 19, 1989, God clarified both the purpose and the nature of Mehu. "There is a purpose for which I brought Mehu, Mighty Nation, onto this earth. Mehu is an independent Nation above all Nations. Heaven is different from Mehu. Heaven is a resting place for the souls of the dead from this earth. Heaven, therefore, should not be likened or compared to Mehu. Mehu is a Nation for cosmic beings, that is, those who live eternally." These distinctions between Mehu and other nations or Churches was one that many people failed to adequately comprehend, however, so the Prophet continued to draw these distinctions in later prophecies and in his teachings.

And, lest it appear that Mehu belongs to the Musama Disco Christo Church or to himself, Prophet Amoaforo also proclaimed through prophecy that "Mehu is nobody's property. It belongs to the Creator called Huhu. It is for both whites and blacks. Mehu is solidly behind the Musama Church at Mozano. Ascended Masters, that is, those who have lived in a Christlike manner and have ascended after death, are all solidly in support of Mehu."

Prophet Amoaforo delivered prophecies annually at Mehu around the end of the year, at the anniversary festivals, and also at other times as the spirit dictated. He once told the Mehu community that "today God is speaking to us face to face as he spoke to many prophets in the olden days". He explained that "some prophecies would be fulfilled instantly or in no time, while others would take years to be fulfilled".

In the annual prophecies and often at mid-year, Prophet Amoaforo also revealed the names of the angels who would guard Mehu for the next interval, either six months, a year, or in some cases five years. These angels and their powers have been discussed in Chapter II. The presence of the angels assured the community that they were under divine protection, so that they could face whatever adversaries they might be required to face.

In the yearly prophecies, the Prophet warned people about the dangers they were likely to face that year or in particular circumstances. He cautioned them against being too desirous of wealth. He told them to be careful about their trading activities and to be cautious about letting strangers stay in their homes. He prophesied about disasters such as ships sinking, airplanes crashing, and road accidents, highway robbery and divorce, corruption in the

Churches and mosques, political corruption and unexpected deaths. He told them that the calamities that might occur were not all due to their fault. He said that some could be explained by the effects of science and technology on modern life.

Above all, the prophecies were realistic about the potential dangers people faced. On farming: "Farm products will not be harvested in abundance as expected; the harvest will be halved. There will not be sufficient rain and sun for the crops to grow. Because of these hard times, man and beast will not be able to sleep well; listlessness and apprehension will haunt many. For three days man may live without obtaining food."

On marriage: "Times will be hard for couples; men and women may leave their partners in search of better ones, but it will be in vain." On overseas travel: "Those who want to travel abroad will not get it easy; immigration laws are being tightened and as a result only a minimum number of persons can travel. They may think by traveling abroad they will acquire properties, but it will not occur as in the past."

On Churches: "Many Churches will become defunct during the year; because the Churches are not from Me, the Lord God, these Churches shall be disgraced". On politics: "Politics will not bring the peace you expect; black as well as white populations shall face political problems. The instability in politics is caused by the fact that everybody is bent on becoming rich. Many people will invest money in politics expecting substantial gain, but they will be disappointed."

On building contractors: "Building contractors will not prosper the way they anticipate; they will execute jobs, but payment will not be forthcoming; therefore, they should be very careful in their business operations." On transport owners: "Transport owners shall make a lot of money. However, the cost of spares and maintenance of their vehicles will be high; this will yield no good returns for transport owners."

On spiritual disease: "The spiritual disease is called Dubra, or HIV/AIDS. Dubra comes with painful and deforming consequences. Prostitutes, both men and women, are advised to be very careful not to contract this disease. Prostitutes are advised to change their way of earning a living; if they should continue in this way, they shall pass away like a flood."

On peace: "Wars, conflicts and the like shall happen in Ghana and abroad, but that cannot improve your living conditions; the antidote is to draw nearer to Me, your Creator. Ask yourselves what you brought into the world and when you die, what can you take away?"

On chieftaincy matters: "Chieftaincy matters shall be unstable this year. Because everybody wants to be rich and prominent, it will bring about chaos. Politicians, both big and small, will be probed and held accountable for their stewardship. This test is like the Israelites' test in the Red Sea; everyone is accountable."

Three prophecies that remained unfulfilled at the Prophet's death are those announcing that God would give the Prophet the gifts of *Nkwa Nsu*, living water, to strengthen them and make them steadfast; *Himankova*, a precious egg-like substance that would be found in the Volta River, and seashore sand that would turn into gold after Prophet Amoaforo performed a special system upon it. When the gifts were not forthcoming, the Prophet explained to the people that they were not yet ready to receive these gifts.

After the yearly prophecies were delivered, the assistants at Mehu consulted the media to corroborate the validity of the prophecies and documented the accuracy of the prophecies for the archives. They drew upon the Ghanaian newspapers, *The Daily Graphic*, *The Mirror*, *The Chronicle*, and *The Statesman* for their evidence. They also cited material on Ghana radio and television programmes when the evidence in print was not available.

At one point, after he had given prophecies at Mehu, Prophet Amoaforo entertained the question, "Why was a lot of reference made to man and his life on earth?" His answer was: "This is because Man is speeding in life's journey on Earth. 'Where are you going?' Man should learn to lead a good life through his worship of God, as well as in his profession, trade and vocation; remember that this world belongs to God; as such you should go through it slowly and carefully. Man gets tired due to his haste in going through this world. The world was created long ago; it is wide, deep and long and there

Prophecy

are a lot of things in it; therefore be careful going through it. A lot of things are thought of by man in this world which should not be the case; man proposes but God disposes.

"Mehu is a great nation which will continue to stir itself. Mehu will continue to fight from now on and will be victorious. Watch out for its works from now on and you will realize that God existed, will exist now and forever. Africans and Europeans will bow to Mehu. Its glory is great. All its plans will work. Blessed is the Lord.

"Do you understand Mehu? No. If you did, you would have worked better for it and sacrificed your life for Mehu's work. Mehu, let your glory descend quickly; we are waiting to see your glory. Devilish spirits rose agaist it but Mehu is victorious. Blessed be the Lord and his angels. Mehu is a nation, not a Church. The Church is included in the things that are found in Mehu. Amen."

The third category of prophecies delivered by Prophet Amoaforo was directed to Akaboha III, Miritaiah Jonah Jehu-Appiah, and to the leadership of the Musama Disco Christo Church. They began on November 9, 1979 and continued until the Prophet's death in 2006. The initial prophecy in this series was a stunning rebuke to the leadership of the Musama Disco Christo Church. Prophet Amoaforo, like the biblical prophets before him, was reluctant to deliver the harsh message he had been given, but according to the prophecy if he did not deliver it he would find himself condemned as well.

So the Prophet attended the 1979 I'Odomey Conference at Mozano, the Church headquarters, to deliver the prophecy in the presence of the whole Musama Disco Christo Church community. He arrived when they were in the midst of a debate about who should be the legitimate heir of the Queenmother, Akatitibi Natholomoa Jehu-Appiah, following her death. This occurred in the seventh year of the reign of Akaboha III, Miritaiah Jonah Jehu-Appiah.

The Prophet discussed the prophecy first with the Senior Prophet, Jimiru Fuah, who accepted it as an authentic prophecy but was not willing to deliver it himself. So the task was left to Jenasman Amoaforo to carry his own "burden," which he did.

In the prophecy, the Lord warned Prophet Amoaforo that if he failed to carry the message, the Lord Himself said He would send a small child to bring the message, but that Jenasman would come to a disgraceful end very soon thereafter. Jenasman then said: "Lord, send me and I will go." Then a voice from heaven said: "Do not take anything away from the message. Cursed be unto you if you add to it and cursed be unto you if you take from it, Amen."

The prophecy stated: "I am the Alpha and Omega – the First and the Last, and I change not. Amen. I the Lord Almighty God, on this day, 6th November 1979 at 3:00 a.m. revealed Myself to My servant Jenasman of Senchi". (The message was delivered to the MDCC on 9th November, 1979.)

"I saw in a vision a great multitude of worshippers. They were singing 'Ma enye yiye, Onyame ma enye yiye', Let all be well, Lord, let all be well in sharp but sweet voices. I heard a voice from Heaven saying: 'The Owner of the Church is coming round about the congregation in a flash'. Then the second voice from Heaven sounded the coming of Nana Miritaiah saying: 'Nana reba o' 'Nana is coming.' He came to sit in a well decorated chair with a blue veil in the background. He then stood up and said: 'Asomdwee Nka Hom', Peace be unto you.

"Instantly the blue veil was torn into two from right to left, revealing another red one in the background. A voice from Heaven said: 'Today is the end of the reign of Miritaiah Jonah Jehu-Appiah. His glory staff in his hand has today been taken from him, because he is no longer doing the will of the Lord God Almighty. Let it be heard that I will no more allow him to use my Church in any way he likes and for his own selfish end. Musama is my Church,' says the Lord.

"'The court case which is facing him now (over succession to the position of Akatitibi) is not my case. Miritaiah is not truly fighting for Me,' says the Lord. 'He should not therefore use or spend the Church's money for this purpose. He, together with his aides and supporters, should therefore cease forthwith with the court case. If there is any real war, I the Lord God Myself will fight. I have angels who are more capable of fighting for Me. They are equally more capable of settling any disputes.'

"'I the Lord God Almighty have on this day abolished the reign of Kings and Queens in the Church. They should all cease to exist in that capacity in the Church. They have all failed to do the Will of the Lord. By their evil advice the Church has been pushed into a ditch. They should no more boast of being a king or queen in the Church, Amen.'

"'Prophetess Daiasarah Forson and her aides should also cease going to court. I, the Lord God, have on this day abolished the position of the Ohemaa (Queen Mother) in the Church. It is no longer necessary,' say I, the Lord God Almighty. Amen. 'The Musama Church should not be sold so cheaply to the public. Amen.'

"Where is the Jehunano Family? What are their functions now? Do they support good or evil? I, the Lord God, demand answers. I, the Lord God, have on this day instructed that the Church should be handed over to Prophet Jimiru Fuah, Senior Prophet, to administer it. Then he should assemble all the elders and the prophets and the pastors at Mozano for three weeks of continuous fasting without salt, fish and pepper and pray for forgiveness of sins. Then will I hear from Heaven and heal them and live among My people once more. If you should harden your hearts and fail to perform this system, Miritaiah will very shortly end his reign in disgrace. Perform a burnt offering, using a white lamb according to the system.'

"Warning:

1. 'If any of you should harden his heart, I, the Lord God will give him only three years to survive and his last days will be worse than the days of Nebuchadnezzer.'

"2. 'If any of you should harden his heart and should institute or enstool a new Ohemaa, that Nana Ohemaa should exist or survive for not more than three years and her last days will be worse than the last days of Nebuchadnezzer and you shall know that I am the Lord and I change not, Amen.'

"3. 'If any of you shall hear His voice today and shall harden his heart and plan to establish a Church of his own, he and his new Church shall be caused to exist for not more than three years and his last days shall be full of disgrace and you shall know that I am the God of your Fathers and I change not, Amen.

"4. 'Prophet Jenasman through whom I am sending my Word should not attempt to establish a Church of his own or a branch of Musama Church for himself. Jenasman will meet total disgrace if he should attempt to do so. Musama Church is no one's personal property. It is my own Church, say I the Lord God Almighty. Amen.'"

Prophet Amoaforo had reason to be concerned about delivering this prophecy because the Akaboha and most of the Pastors and Prophets who led the Church rejected it. Some accused him of blasphemy, abomination and lies, and they hurled insults on him for hours. In short, he was accused of being guilty of the charges he brought against the Akaboha III. He was denied the opportunity to defend himself and was fined a sheep. When Chief Nana Gyima of Asante Asokore and Elder J.S.T. Addy of the Chorkor Musama Disco Christo Church spoke out against the treatment of Prophet Amoaforo, they too were insulted.

The Adontenhene, Nana Kweku Acquah, warned the Conference and Akaboha III to be careful because, he said, he knew who Prophet Amoaforo was, having lived with him for years at Koforidua. He warned that, in condemning Prophet Amoaforo, they were playing with fire, or were acting like children playing with a sharp knife. He predicted they would live to regret it.

Among those hurling the insults was Tupamaica Eburey, Chief Linguist of the Church, who said the Prophet would have been beheaded if this were the old days. Anna Amo, and Silisiana Araba Aseradu who sprinkled florida water around where the prophet was standing as if to fumigate the place, also participated in the condemnation of Prophet Amoaforo. The Prophet warned them that God would repay them in kind for their actions.

Prophet Amoaforo then went in search of a sheep and returned the next day to present it, with the help of Prophet Kwasi Mensah. It was slaughtered and shared at Mozano. A piece was also sent to the Prophet as custom demands, but he refused to accept it. Next, the Conference suspended the Prophet from engaging in Church activities. He was not shaken at all, because he said he knew the ball was going to bounce back from the wall and hit them hard.

During his suspension, Prophet Amoaforo visited the home of a couple at Dawenya. There the spirits of the Akaboha I and II, and the Akatitibi I visited him in a dream and told him that they had assigned him his mission in the Musama Disco Christo Church, and no one else could take it away. They assured him of their support

Prophecy

and his impending victory, and encouraged him not to lose hope but to fight on. The couple reanointed his head physically with special oil that trickled down his body. A tenant in the same house, whose thumb had been swollen for two weeks, touched the trickling oil and was healed instantly.

On June 4, 1984, Musama Disco Christo Church records show that a fire broke out at Mozano and burned the palace built by Akaboha II, Matapoly Moses Jehu-Appiah. Unfortunately all the early records of the MDCC were burned in this fire. Apparently, the fire was interpreted by some in the Church as a punishment for its treatment of Prophet Amoaforo.

Subsequently, in March of 1985, Rev. Moses Nyarkoh sent the following message to Prophet Amoaforo. "It was Wednesday at 6:00 or 7:00 in the morning when I received this message that Prophet J. K. Amoaforo should be clean in heart and forgive everybody for what has happened between him and anybody else and forget the past. He also prophesied that a letter would be sent to the Prophet informing him that he would be called in two months' time to take up his work again. I was taken to a hall where many prophets were sitting and they showed me Prophet J. K. Amoaforo's seat. I came to tell him all that had happened this morning."

This prophecy of Rev. Nyarkoh came to pass when, shortly thereafter, Rev. J.K.K. Bagyinah was sent to Senchi by the Akaboha III to summon the Prophet to meet with the Akaboha at Mozano. The Prophet went there and was told by the Akaboha III that he wanted the Prophet to forget about what happened and to "smoke the peace pipe." The Prophet's suspension from the Musama Disco Christo Church was lifted and he was given a mandate to continue his missionary work, since God was his provider and helper, his guide and protector.

Finally, the fulfillment of the prophecies that Prophet Amoaforo made to the Akaboha III in 1979 began to come to resolution. On February 25, 2003, Prophet Amoaforo revealed a list of Pastors, Prophets and workers in the Musama Disco Christo Church that should be cut off from the Church by the beginning of January, 2004. He also prophesied that fierce lightning would start from the Mazpiola in Mozano, continuing through the Jehunano Temple and the Holy Place, to the Queenmother's Bonasaidom house, and finally to Nana's palace into the citronella plantation. Finally, he revealed that if things continued the way they were going, Mehu would be taken from the Musama Disco Christo Church by 1 January, 2004.

On the morning of June 9, 2003, Miritaiah Jonah Jehu-Appiah was removed from office by the Elders of the Musama Disco Christo Church. They had been convinced by testimonies from leading Musama members that the Akaboha's immoral behaviour was not worthy of the Head of the Church, and therefore he should no longer serve in that capacity.

On the same day at 8:20 a.m. Prophet Jenasman Amoaforo delivered the following prophecy: "The angel *Shiomaama* has been delegated to take charge of the 16th anniversary celebration at Mehu. His shining glory is like the morning sun. He has come to change the mourning of the afflicted into laughter. He has come to reveal a lot of things and everybody will be happy in life. Musama is a good Church, and is capable of doing everything through God's power from now on. Mighty beings have fallen because of Mehu. God is victorious. The Musama Disco Christo Church does not belong to anybody. I the Lord possess it. The Musama Disco Christo Church is on my heart. If you play with it you will be in trouble."

Shortly after noon on the same day, June 9, 2003, a team of six Executive members of the Musama Disco Christo Church arrived at Mehu from Mozano. When their arrival was announced, they were ushered in to the Prophet who welcomed them. After prayers, they were asked to state their mission. They formally apologized for not accepting the prophecy of 1979 and thus the Church had found itself in a period of terrible crisis. They also provided a sheep as a replacement for the one that Prophet Amoaforo was required to bring to Mozano in 1979.

Prophet Amoaforo accepted the sheep and asked Prophet Ankomah to pray, there and then, to seal it. He announced the system to be performed with the sheep at Mehu by Prophet Ankomah. That Church father prayed penitently for forgiveness at 1:00 p.m. while the sheep was held on the ground. Those present said it was a solemn moment.

Prophecy

After the prayers, white powder was sprinkled on all in the Mehu. Offerings were made and the delegation departed from Mehu, leaving the sheep behind. Then the Prophet advised them to behave well because there would be victory ahead. A few questions were asked and answered. After that, prayers were said for the team's departure to Mozano about 1:30 p.m., June 9, 2003.

The prophecy Prophet Amoaforo delivered on June 21, 2003 at 11:45 a.m. stated: "I the Lord do not find anything wrong in the realm. I am with you in the heavens and earth, in mountains, everywhere. Musama is my Church and it is my heart. I advise you to be calm. You are victorious, I assure you.

"Perform a system as follows. Slaughter a sheep and prepare food – rice and all – share and give some out to the people. You will get rid of trouble and have rest from your troubles. The battle is ended. Prophet J. K. Amoaforo is here supporting you. Be careful of the people you move with. Use drums and other musical instruments to praise God after the battle is over. There are angels fighting for the Musama Disco Christo Church at Mozano now, on your behalf."

In the meantime, however, even after the reconciliation between Prophet Amoaforo and the Musama leadership, Prophet Amoaforo continued to deliver prophecies containing references to the situation at Mozano, offering support to the elders and members, and strengthening their belief in the power of Mehu.

On Tuesday, July 8, 2003 at 1:15 p.m. the Prophet offered them encouragement to continue their belief in the power of Mehu, despite the fact that the Akaboha III refused to accept the new leadership of the Church. He prophesied, "So many good things are coming to Mehu. Because you are not on the same level, you cannot envision it. All will come true and you will all say 'God, you are truthful'. Discouragement and hindrance are the plans of the enemies against Mehu, but all will come to naught."

On December 20, 2003, Prophet Amoaforo reported that "the astral world has been concerned about the crisis in the Musama Church. The Seenim members should have put on their uniforms and demonstrated in the town to show that they do not want the Akaboha III and his mother anymore." He also informed them that "an iron wall has been erected around the whole town of Mozano.

It has 77 gates or outlets. Miritaiah will be pulled out through one of them."

On December 24, 2003, "Prophet J. K. Amoaforo traveled to the astral world. He was instructed to summon the following people to Mozano for a meeting: Nana Twafohene, Nana Adontenhene and Miritaiah. During the session Miritaiah was told by Prophet J. K. Amoaforo that God had destooled him and his mother and that the Musama Disco Christo Church would be headed by a leader selected by God. 'No more chieftaincy affairs in the Church?' Miritaiah asked. 'Who amongst them has not committed a crime before?' Miritaiah said he was not prepared to leave Mozano and their properties there, but God has his own plans awaiting him."

There was continuing concern about the situation at Mozano in early February, evidenced by the prophecies that Prophet Amoaforo delivered on February 19, 2004: "I am Alpha and Omega. I have been in existence forever. No one knows my beginning or end. The Musama Disco Christo Church is mine, not from man. I have a purpose for establishing it on this earth and it is going to be fulfilled.

"The following system is to be performed as a response to this prophecy: 'Every member at this station and its environs should take the holy bath. Palm fronds should be spread all over the yard at Mehu. Prayers should be offered by members for seven days, morning and evening, each holding a lighted candle.'

"Since I have kept mute, you think I am like you. Even when I have not stirred myself, the Musama Disco Christo Church is a sharp frightening Sword. Therefore let all fear the God who established the Church. Let everybody, old or young, obey the laws of the Church. Let no one take the Church as his own property. The Church is for the whole world.

"If you will obey my laws, and do my wish, I will provide for all your needs. I will give *Nkwa Nsu*, 'the water of life,' heavenly names and money. Nothing will be missing from them. Obey my laws and there will be no trouble

"System: Fast for seven days. The first three days, ask for forgiveness of sins. On the fourth to the seventh days, ask God to disclose the purpose of the establishment of the Musama Disco Christo Church, and ask God to stir Himself. Prepare a love feast of bread and water

Prophecy

and all should eat and drink. Let the prophets and elders organize the people to sweep and clean the town in order to heal it. Prophet J.K Amoaforo should sanctify stones to be spread in the town to heal and sanctify it. Let the prophets pray over the stones. The prayer should be that God should raise his hands over Mozano and subdue his enemies.

"When the 1979 prophecies were sent, did you act on them? No. That is why there is trouble. Let us fear God. Where is the Jehunano family? The First and Second Committees, the chiefs and queens? What is their work? I, God, promise that from now to January 1, 2005, I will send members both old and young, money and all your needs to the Church.

"The Musama Disco Christo Church is from God. Let us fear Him. The Musama Church will never fail. It will be victorious. It is not a Church for the poor. I will give you money. I have a lot to tell you. After the fasting, give an offering to cover the expenses and the remaining balances should be sent to the bank account. God will send money into it. God will give the Church capital. Let proper arrangements be made to save the balance."

This prophecy was followed a few days later, on 23rd February, 2004, by another stinging prophecy against what was going on at Mozano: "Peace be unto you. Amen. As it was in the beginning, so it is now and for ever. I have already told you to fear the Lord and obey the laws and I will give you everything. I the Lord will turn sand, water, leaves, air into gold for the Musama Disco Christo Church. So obey the laws and I will give you everything.

"Do not handle the Church as a plaything. The Musama Disco Christo Church is independent, not the poor but our doings have brought us to this level, so let all fear the Lord to glorify Jemisimiham. When we started last week, I sent you four hundred thousand Cedis. Give two hundred thousand Cedis to the Jehunano elder men and one hundred thousand Cedis to the Jehunano elder women.

"Once you leave here start the system immediately. Those who cannot fast should not be included. Thus says the Lord, I God neither die nor slumber. I will glorify Africa. The whole world belongs to me. The purpose of sending Jehu, Jesus and others is to take you to heaven, not to enrich yourselves. God is going to provide money for us, so let us be careful of our ways.

"From now on, prayers should be intensified. Leave your wayward lives behind. Old and young should do as I command. If not, your services will be for nothing. So I have sent the Angel Huhumahuumahuu ("Alpha and Omega") to come and assist you. So let all say, 'God, we will obey your laws'.

"The prophecy of Prophet Jemisimiham, Nathalomoa, the Queen Mother, and the Akasibeena, Prince Matapoly Moses Jehu-Appiah, will be fulfilled. The sign of that is the 400,000 Cedis I sent to you after last week's prophecy. 300,000 Cedis is for the Jehunano family, 200,000 Cedis for men and 100,000 Cedis for the elder women."

"The Church is not the property of anybody, from the elephant to the ant. Let proper arrangements be made for the progress of the Church. Do not worry about money. I am sending avenues for healing which will bring you income. Let all work towards that to perform wonders. You will say that the God of Jehu is a warrior.

"Let the Thursday vigil and Friday System be of importance to you. Peace be unto the Musama Disco Christo Church, Africa and the whites. Let this be enough for you. Consult the Senior Prophet on every step you will take. This year should be a good and prosperous one for you."

On December 25, 2004, Prophet Amoaforo assured the Musama Disco Christo Church that God had released two angels, *Sedra* from the 44th planet and *Onaana* from the 55th planet, to fight the Church crisis. The prophecy continued: "The leaders of the angels who are released will work from the opposite directions East and West at the beginning of the year to meet and finish the work [resolving the crisis at Mozano] by the middle of the year.

"Next year, the Musama Disco Christo Church will stir itself. Thursday vigil is to be revived and intensified. Friday prayers should also be treated with the same importance as Thursday vigil. The present crisis in the Church is like a cork under water in a river. It will certainly pop up at the appropriate time. Do not be troubled about this crisis. I, the *Abedu* angel, Alpha and Omega, have arrived. Amen."

Prophecy

On March 16, 2006, shortly before his death, Prophet Amoaforo received another prophecy for the community, indicating another crisis for the Musama Disco Christo Church: "A great power has descended to take charge of the Musama Disco Christo Church. Nobody, Pastor or Prophet, no matter your rank, should go to the Holy Place and touch the Ark. The power of the Ark is from God. Anyone who touches the Ark will go mad. Prayers should be offered in front of the Holy Place. The old things have passed. The power that has descended is called Hibratoni, meaning no respecter of persons.

"From now on, anybody who engages in immoral activities, drinking, or womanizing, will be cut off. One elder will die. Don't use your own power to do things; otherwise you will die. God says that because He is quiet you think He is not aware of the recent happenings. God will descend with fire and thunder to stir the Musama Church.

"Who is man at all? Those who will run away will do so. Others who should die will also die. The immoral behaviour started long ago. That is the reason for sending Prophet Jenasman Kwadwo Amoaforo and my angels to destool the Akaboha III. *Nkwa nsu* and heavenly names will be given. A three-man committee should be set up to run the affairs of the Church until God chooses someone else to head the Church."

About a week later, on March 21, 2006, God gave Prophet Amoaforo another prophecy: "Nobody from the ant to the elephant should touch the Ark. Nobody should open the Ark. The Ark is the power of the Musama Disco Christo Church. Some people have made up their minds to see inside the Ark. The Church does not belong to anyone to use it as he or she wishes. God says it is His Church; immoral activities are the plans of the devil.

"The incoming power is going to work wonderfully for all to marvel over. The throne is not a family one; it is from Me, the Almight God, says the Lord. Pastors, Prophets and leaders of the Church should be very careful. Do you understand the Musama Disco Christo Church at all? If you do, you will not behave like this.

"*Nkwa Nsu* and heavenly names will all come, if you stop your immoral activities. The elders of the Church should be bold to tell the truth and not fear anyone. The devil has gripped the members through immoral activities, but God's power is great and has sustained the Church. Most of the supporters are looking for posts. We have to see to the upliftment of the Church. The power has everything: wealth, prosperity for the Church and its members. Do not play with the Church. May Peace be unto you. I am with you until the end of the world. I am Alpha and Omega. If these immoral acts are not stopped, no miracles or wonders can be done in the Church."

Despite Prophet Amoaforo's persistence in delivering the prophecies he was given, however, Miritaiah Jonah Jehu-Appiah, Akaboha III, refused to accept the decision of the Musama Elders to remove him from office in 2003 and appealed to the Ghana Court to settle the matter. The Court, after a number of appeals and counterappeals, ruled in favor of the Musama Disco Christo Church and not the Akaboha III.

The Interim Management Committee that had assumed responsibility for the Church in 2003 installed as the new General Head Prophet, Moknajeeba Fiifi Jehu-Appiah, son of the late Prophet Matapoly Moses Jehu-Appiah, Akaboha II. He was given full authority over the Musama Disco Christo Church, effective December 29, 2007.

Meanwhile, after Prophet Jenasman Kwadwo Amoaforo died in June, 2006, without seeing the final settlement of the Mozano crisis, further prophecies to the Musama Church in the names of Prophet Matapoly Moses Jehu-Appiah, Prophet Amoaforo and the angel Michael were delivered by Prophet J. R. Odoom, Prophet Amoaforo's successor at Mehu.

When Prophet Jemisimiham Jehu-Appiah and Kwadwo Amoaforo first met, the Akaboha invited the young missionary of the Musama Disco Christo Church to join him in his mission to fight in the battle for Africa, and to work to complete the building of the Church. Prophet Amoaforo accepted this invitation and worked throughout his life to fulfill these missions. He labored tirelessly to bring the message of Musama to Africans. He worked for the completion of the building of the Musama Disco Christo Church, first by spreading the Church throughout a large part of Ghana, and then by fighting relentlessly to maintain the integrity of the Church and its leadership. Perhaps the latter task was even more challenging than the former.

Prophecy

The fullment of Prophet Amoaforo's prophecies against the Akaboha III, Miritaiah Jonah Jehu-Appiah, came with the installation of a new General Head Prophet in the person of Moknajeeba Fiifi Jehu-Appiah. Thanks to Prophet Amoaforo's unrelenting labours to honour his commitments to Prophet Jemismiham Jehu-Appiah and to God, the Musama Disco Christo Church can now look forward to a sound and stable future.

Chapter Five

Theology

Jenasman Kwadwo Amoaforo developed a complex theological system during the course of his life as a Prophet of the Musama Disco Church. What makes Prophet Amoaforo's theology unique is a creative weaving of traditions from Akan culture, the Bible, Musama belief and practice and his own spiritual experiences into a coherent theological system.

As a young man, Prophet Amoaforo appears not to have been an especially devout Presbyterian, the church to which his parents belonged. But by the time he encountered Prophet Jemisimiham Jehu Appiah, he had just had some unusual spiritual experiences that initially he did not fully understand. First, he found himself involuntarily engaged in a ritual that resulted in the healing of the wife of his master tailor. Second, he had a profound set of encounters with two angels who strengthened him for his future mission as a prophet and healer. These experiences, along with absorbing Akan perspectives since childhood, were foundational for Prophet Amoaforo's theological development.

Akan belief in the connectedness and interrelatedness of Divinity, spirit world, ancestors, human and other sentient communities, and the whole cosmic system informed Prophet Amoaforo's perspective in fundamental ways. This understanding of the relationship between human beings and the universe, for one example, made his relationships with angels and his travels to the astral world quite comprehensible. Often humans turn to the angels for their many needs, whether physical, material or spiritual, and for the healing of ills within the social community, between individuals and the community, the natural environment or the ancestors.

Although he was raised in a devout Christian family, Prophet

Amoaforo may not have been comfortable with a religion that offered only spiritual salvation, not deliverance from all the oppressions experienced in human life. He most likely learned his mature understanding of Christianity from Prophet Jemisimiham Jehu-Appiah and his Musama church colleagues who had reinterpreted missionary Christianity into an African religion that responded to the full range of human experiences.

Prophet Amoaforo came to understand that the God of the Hebrew Bible was not only a warrior and protector of His people, demanding justice, but was also compassionate in response to human needs. He regarded the Jesus of the Christian Scripture as a healer who provided a powerful model of mercy, compassion and practical assistance that Africans associate with the idea of salvation. However, he did not view Jesus as divine, as most African and other orthodox Christian theologies do. Rather, he believed that Jesus came as an avatar to show us the qualities of the divine in the human world for the benefit of mankind.

Prophet Amoaforo's theology evolved and was revealed through his missionary activity, and through his work at the Senchi Healing and Retreat Centre, where his healings, exorcisms and prophecies were carefully documented since 1980. Prophet Amoaforo also expressed his theology through the physical structures he was guided to design for the Mehu Healing and Retreat Centre and the incorporation of cosmic representations that he had seen in the astral realm.

The wall paintings at Mehu include depictions of biblical texts that Prophet Amoaforo illustrated in the wall art. The representations of the spiritual leaders – biblical, Musama and religious leaders from various traditions – that influenced him, reflect his view of the validity and inclusivity of all religious expressions, a view to which the Musama church was also committed.

The cosmic symbols that abound in the physical structure of Mehu represent Prophet Amoaforo's heavenly travels and revelations, combined with his Akan knowledge of the considerable influence of the planets, sun, moon, and stars on the lives of people on earth. In the Akan tradition, an acute awareness of the physical world is also related to an appreciation of the nature spirits that inhabit it. Symbols such as the sun, moon, stars, and other celestial phenomena are also frequently associated, in both the Hebrew and the Christian Scriptures, with a heightened eschatological expectation of God's judgment on wickedness.

At Mehu, Malachi 4:2 and 1 Corinthians 15:40 are used to confirm the significance of celestial symbols both as heavenly realities and as expressions of the confidence that believers can have in God's mercy and compassion if they repent and ask for deliverance. The red and yellow suns in one part of Mehu call devotees to repentance both in the physical space between the two suns and in the interval before the end of the world.

One area of the shrine also recalls for Musama members the prophecy made by Akaboha I, Jemisimiham Jehu-Appiah in 1930 when the community set out to proclaim the message that the Second Coming of the Lord was near. The prophecy stated: "A day is coming, when the whole world will be greatly alarmed by this phenomenon. At one sunset, the whole atmosphere will turn awfully red till midnight. This will be followed by dew which will drizzle like rain till six o'clock in the morning.

"Then a great flashing light will appear in the skies in the form of a circle, and this will immediately be followed by total eclipse. This dreadful darkness will last for twelve hours. Seven days after these signs, there will be a strong and thunderous rain and an earthquake which will last for three days, day and night. Then a piercing cold will come, killing many sinners – especially murderers, witches, thieves, robbers, sorcerers, drunkards, fornicators, litigants, idolaters and others.

"When the first three signs are observed, the chief or ruler of every town or village should order all kinds of talismans, fetishes and occult shrines to be gathered at the outskirts of the town or village and be burnt. Then all the townsfolk should gather at an open space and pray for forgiveness of sin and deliverance. There is no medicine or any precaution to this ravaging cold other than prayers to God" (Opoku, *Musama*).

Thus, the very existence of Mehu is an announcement of the end of the world and the coming judgment. In addition, the prophecies that were revealed to the Prophet, like those of the Hebrew prophets, Jesus, and the apocalyptic seers of the Christian Testament, pronounced judgment against wickedness. They were directed toward repudiating public corruption in both political and religious systems, as well as in people's personal lives. They warned of the need for repentance, which was reinforced annually when global and local events that occurred during the previous year were recounted to demonstrate the accuracy of the Prophet's prophecies.

Cosmic symbols at Mehu were not just eschatological warnings, however. As has been noted above, the stars in the structures of Mehu, which were thought to rival in number those of the heavens, also symbolized God's glory. Certain clusters of stars at Mehu had specific referents, such as one group of twelve stars that symbolize the twelve apostles, five stars for the five letters in the name, Jesus, three stars that represent the wise men, and another three that commemorate the three women at Jesus' tomb. Other stars represent the heavenly hosts well known in the biblical tradition, the *Cherubim* and *Seraphim*.

The Prophet often assured devotees that the angels were given to them by God for their protection against the principalities and powers of darkness that also inhabit the human world. Ephesians 6:12 witnessed to the reality of the evil powers, saying "for our struggle is against the cosmic powers of this present darkness, against the spiritual forces of evil in the heavenly places." However, Psalm 91:9-11, referred to in several places on the walls of Mehu, assures them of the protection of the angels in their struggle: "Because you have made the Lord your refuge, the Most High your dwelling place, no evil shall befall you, no scourge come near your tent, for he will command his angels concerning you to guard you in all your ways."

Biblical narratives are painted on the walls of Mehu to illuminate God's plan for humanity and also the ways in which God has already worked on behalf of humans. Devotees are reminded of this by a vivid wall painting of the Genesis creation accounts that affirm the goodness of creation, the role of humans in the world, and the necessity of good works (Genesis 1:24-28, 31; 2:8-9, 17; 3:19, 23; 6:6; Exodus 20:9).

The wandering of the chosen people of Israel and the difficulties they faced despite their election resonated with the history of the early Musama Disco Church. These were themes that are found

Theology

often in the art at Mehu. Despite their covenantal relationship with God, represented by paintings of Abraham on an entrance to the Sala Mehu, the giving of the Ten Commandments, and references to Exodus 19:4-25, 20:1-18; 32:15-16, Israel had to endure the hardships of slavery in Egypt, a precarious journey of escape from captivity, and years of wandering in the desert with danger threatening on every side (Deuteronomy 2:1-30).

Another painting portrays Joshua in battle the day the sun stood still and makes other references to Joshua 10:6-15; 12:7-24; and 14:1-5. Judges 3:8-13, however, describes the people turning to other gods after the death of Joshua and warns the Mehu community not to become complacent and lax in their beliefs and practices.

Even after their establishment in Canaan, the people of Israel had to struggle against adversity, symbolized in a painting that shows Samson struggling with the lion (Judges 14:5-9). But adversity also came to the people as a result of the infidelity of their leaders. One painting shows Samuel anointing Saul and cites texts describing Saul's subsequent disobedience, which caused God to take the kingship away from him (1 Samuel 9:11, 13:5-14, 14:47-52, 15:1-35), and David's lament over the deaths of Saul and Jonathan (2 Samuel 1:23).

Both God's and the community's fidelity are represented in two sets of five stars symbolizing the five smooth stones with which David slew Goliath (1 Samuel 17:40) and in the reference to the deliverance of the three young men from the fiery furnace (Daniel 3:1-30). Similarly, Mehu's references to the Psalms testify to the infidelities of Israel, despite its covenant with God, and also to God's promise of continued guidance and protection when the people repented (Isaiah 58:1-14; Jeremiah 9:24; Psalms 3; 37:3; 88).

Representations of Jesus's life, death, and resurrection into glory also have a prominent place at Mehu. A large painting of Mary with the infant Jesus dominates one of its entrances. The significance of Jesus' birth is indicated by reference to Luke 2: 25-30, which is Simeon's thanksgiving that the promise of a Messiah had been fulfilled in this child. Jesus's mission is described in terms reminiscent of Prophet Amoaforo's own mission: Jesus went through Galilee, teaching in synagogues, proclaiming the good news of the

Kingdom, and curing every disease and every sickness among the people (Matthew 4:23).

An invitation to explore Jesus's identity further is offered by the citation in the Mehu literature of John 1:46: "Nathaniel said, 'Can anything good come out of Nazareth?' Philip said, 'Come and See,' as an invitation to see the power of God demonstrated in the Musama Disco Christo Church. At both Mehu and Musama, the power of Jesus is represented through healing depictions and through prophecy.

A painting of Jesus teaching from a boat with a large group of followers dressed in contemporary attire fills a wall at Mehu. There are also references to John 14:6 and 3:16, disclosing the Christology of Mehu: "Jesus said, 'I am the way, and the truth, and the life. No one comes to the Father except through me' and 'For God so loved the world that he gave his only son, so that everyone who believes in him may not perish but may have eternal life.'" Other passages from John's gospel are also used at Mehu to affirm the significance of Jesus and the importance of his role in guiding the faithful: "If you abide in me, and my words abide in you, ask for whatever you wish, and it will be done for you" (15:7) and "You will know the truth and the truth will make you free" (8:32). John 10:14 underscores the point: "I am the good shepherd. I know my own and my own know me."

Many symbols and scenes of events from Jesus's passion and death are also found at Mehu. A wall painting at the entrance to the area for repentance shows the agony of Jesus in Gethsemane. In another painting, Jesus wears a crown of thorns. In one area, three crosses are erected, one for Jesus and the other two for the thieves put to death with him. Jesus's victory over death in the resurrection is celebrated by Huma, the largest cross that is painted in red and white spirals to symbolize both blood and victory. The heart of Jesus pierced with a knife is depicted on the cross, but on its top is a gold crown showing Jesus' ultimate victory over death, a promise to believers about their own destiny as well.

Other symbolic and representational images of Jesus's victory are to be seen in the "Victory Stone" and in paintings of Jesus labeled "Rock of Ages"; with a halo; with arms outstretched and pots of flame, probably representing the angels, on each side of him; and as the "War Captain." Another painting of Jesus is inscribed, "In the name of our Lord Jesus Christ." However, Mehu literature not only confirms the victory of Jesus, it also promises the faithful that they will share in his victory in the not-too-distant future. Matthew 24:14 says, "And this good news of the kingdom will be proclaimed throughout the world, as a testimony to all the nations; and then the end will come." Revelation 22:12 is also cited in this regard: "See, I am coming soon; my reward is with me, to repay according to everyone's work." And hymn number 272 in the Methodist Hymnal used at Mehu proclaims: "Jesus shall reign wherever the sun shines... His kingdom shall stretch from shore to shore."

In addition to the biblical references and allusions, there are many references to the Musama Disco Christo Church in the paintings and representations at Mehu. Most prominent are the portraits of the first three male leaders and the two female leaders of the Musama Disco Christo Church: Akaboha I, Jemisimiham Jehu-Appiah; Akaboha II, Mathapoly Moses Jehu-Appiah; Akaboha III, Miritaiah Jonah Jehu-Appiah; Akatitibi I, Natholomoa Jehu-Appiah; and Akatitibi II, Mathabinaia Jehu-Appiah. The portrait of the first resident minister from the Musama Disco Christo Church at Mehu, Reverend Martin Luther King Jehu-Appiah, is also prominently displayed.

Mehu also contains a number of symbols that recall the history of the Musama Disco Christo Church. They include the double-edged sword representing the two founders of the church; war weapons which suggest the church's self-identification as "the Army of the Cross of Christ" (though since the Benso crisis early in the church's history, it understands itself as a spiritual rather than an actual army); and scissors and a blade, symbolizing cleanliness and suffering. Airplanes refer to Prophet Amoaforo's spiritual journeys; a red fez and sandals, his spiritual commitment and his dedication to the work of Musama as a traveling prophet and healer.

While there are a number of religious traditions woven into Prophet Amoaforo's theology, it also differs in a number of respects from orthodox Christian teaching and practice as well as from those of the Musama Disco Christo Church. Drawing upon the Akan tradition, Prophet Amoaforo understood that the Creator, known as *Odomankoma Oboadee* and by other names, is essentially a spirit. Unlike

Theology

the traditional Christian theological view, the universe is believed to have had a definite beginning but no clear end. The universe is one reality with two aspects, visible and invisible. The reality of the universe is reflected in everything that exists, including angels, demons, humans, nature and the heavenly and earthly Mehu.

The divinity, *Onyame*, stands in a relationship of both transcendence and immanence to the created order. All other beings are subordinate to the Creator: spirits, benevolent or malevolent (in Prophet Amoaforo's system, these are the angels and demons); humans; objects in nature; and the power or energy that permeates the universe.

Prophet Amoaforo provided an elaborate account of the creation of the world as occurring in a hierarchical order. First, there was God. Next in order came the *Narsinas* and the *Adras*, celestial beings that existed before the creation of the world. They lived on the 335th and 334th planets and served as deputies and ministers of God. They received petitions from suffering humanity that were sent to God by the Jahuus and the angels who followed them in the order of creation. The Prophet insisted that the Ten Commandments were given to Moses on the Kandara Mountain, where the *Narsinas* lived, not at Sinai, as reported in the Hebrew Scriptures.

Finally came the creation of the planetary system (sun, moon, stars, and other planetary beings), of sea animals and birds, and, last, of land animals and humans. In another context, Prophet Amoaforo explained that the animals were "called," not "created" as man was. Only humans were given the breath of God, which meant humans were created in God's own image. It is only if humans live pure lives, however, that they are superior to the animals. Otherwise, the hierarchy is reversed. Enmity between humans and animals occurred only after the flood, when humans were told to eat the flesh of animals.

Prophet Amoaforo's account of creation does not wholly conform to the traditional Akan conception of creation or to the process of creation described in the Scriptures. Both believe that God is the creator of heaven and the universe and all things in it. But Prophet Amoaforo rejects the biblical understanding that God was eternal and assumes that God himself came into being at a particular point by

Theology

self-generation. This is a notion also present in some ancient Egyptian theologies. Both the biblical tradition and Prophet Amoaforo agree that the worlds were not made out of any pre-existing material but out of nothing, by the divine word. The *Narsinus* and the *Adras* also fall within the category of creations from nothing. Human beings, however, do not.

Prophet Amoaforo gave a unique account of the creation of human beings that also differs from the two biblical accounts in Genesis. He believed that the Creator collected dust from the ground and laid it down without form. Then rain fell and worms appeared; ants and also other creatures emerged as well. After a time, human heads and hands and other body parts also emerged from the dust. It took some three hundred years to complete the creation of human beings. Then God breathed eternal fire into the human form and it became a human being.

The Prophet also explained that "the earth has a lot of impurities in it, which is why we have to die, so as to allow the impure parts of the body to be cleansed and wither away. Only then can we return to another holy planet, to heaven, in the purest form. The journey of humans to heaven is thus like the cleansing of gold, which is usually collected from dirt" and needs to be purified.

In Akan belief and also in the Prophet's view and in Christianity, man shares in the dependence of the rest of the creation on the Creator. Even in making nature serve him, human beings have to serve nature, tend it, and bring it to fruition (Genesis 2:15). In the Christian tradition and in Prophet Amoaforo's thought, nature is not simply a neutral framework or background for human life. Between nature and humanity there are deep and mysterious bonds. Nature is regarded in the Scriptures as rejoicing in the events that lead to humanity's redemption (Psalms 96, 10-13; Isaiah 35:4).

The Akan have several traditional explanations for the present state of human existence. One narrative recounts that in the beginning, God dwelt on the earth and interacted with humans, but they disturbed God by their behaviour. Another story tells of a woman who kept hitting God with the handle of her pestle as she was pounding *fufu*, a starchy food staple in Ghana, and so God withdrew from human reach. So the old woman advised her children to stack

Theology

up their mortars, one on top of the other, and then to remove the bottom mortar from the stack, causing all the other mortars to come crashing to the ground. This story has been understood traditionally to mean that it is impossible for humans to reach God without an intermediary, or even to fully know God.

The Akan do not normally address their prayers directly to God, but ultimately all prayers do reach God. Rather, they invoke the assistance of the spirits and of the ancestors, the living-timeless, whose concern for the community and its well-being continues after death, since there is a need for intermediaries between the spirit and the human worlds.

The traditional Akan account of human development differs from the Biblical version. (Opoku, *WATR*, 94-100) It regards humans as having four essential elements of which the most important is the *okra* or soul, the undying part of humans given by the Creator. In this regard, Akan theology and Christian theology are similar. Death indicates a return of the *okra* to its source, where it continues to live beyond death. When the *okra* is ready for birth or rebirth, it begs leave to depart from its Creator and it receives its mission in life, *nkrabea*, which is fixed in advance and is unalterable. The realization of this destiny on earth is called *obra* or *abrabo*.

The other three essential elements given by the Creator are: *sunsum*, the disposition and intelligence of a person; *ntoro*, which is transmitted from a father to his children and helps to account for their inherited characteristics; *mogya*, blood, which is given by a mother to her child and establishes a physiological bond between them.

Prophet Amoaforo was also familiar with the concept of the contract made between God and the person before birth. He said that at the pre-birth meeting, the *okra* tells God what it will do to glorify the Creator and how, where, and when it will die and return to be reunited with *Odomankoma*. The Creator then approves, signs, and seals the attestation, and presents the child with an attested copy of it at the time of departing to the earth realm.

Prophet Amoaforo discussed the contract that he himself had with God before he descended. He agreed with God that he would become the leader of the angels causing thunder. Apparently he also agreed to work with the Akaboha I, Jemisimiham Jehu-Appiah, to team up with him and to kindle the Musama Disco Christo Church. He said he would have been able to do this even if he had not become a member of the Musama Christo Disco Church.

In the Akwamu area, his contract included the erection of the *Makatapi* monument as a blessing for the area and to assist in gaining independence from Britain for the Gold Coast. He also had the responsibility as part of his contract to encourage industry in the area, including the Akosombo Hydroelectric Power Project, the Volta Dam, and the Adomi Bridge, and in the development of the industries and amenities necessary for the prosperity of the area.

When asked later in his life how much of the contract he made in the spiritual realm had been completed and how much still remained to be done, Prophet Amoaforo said that he had completed most of the contract, but that the angels did not inform him about what remained to be done until the time come for him to do it. When he was asked what part of the contract he was fulfilling at that particular time, the Prophet stated that he was trying to turn sand into gold and going into the Volta River to extract the *himankova*, an egg-like substance, with the glass and spoon he had been given when he initially received healing and prophetic power.

Another major disagreement with the Bible, but not necessarily with Christian theology, in the Prophet's theology centered upon the Christian interpretation of Adam and Eve's offense against God, the Creator, and its consequences. According to the Bible, the fall of humanity was the result of the sin of disobedience against God's command in the Garden of Eden, as recorded in Genesis 3. Two striking wall paintings at Mehu illustrate the departure of Adam and Eve from the Garden. Following their transgression, they were driven from their home, the man to till the ground by the sweat of his brow and the woman to bring forth children in sorrow and pain. The climax of their punishment was death. According to the apostle Paul, from that day onward death was passed on as a punishment to all human beings, since all humans sinned in Adam's sin and therefore all will die (1 Corinthians 15:2).

Prophet Amoaforo, however, disagreed with the perspective of the Bible on what constituted the failure of the first humans and its consequences. He insisted that Adam's action of eating fruit, as

Theology

described in Genesis 3, followed the divine plan. In other words, before Adam was created, God knew that such a thing would happen in the course of human existence in the Garden of Eden, and it did. The Prophet believed that it was sexual intercourse, not the eating of fruit, that was the offense, because it was a violation of God's command. Thus, human wrongdoing made it impossible for humans to fulfill their destiny.

The punishment that Adam and Eve received, according to Prophet Amoaforo, was being expelled from the astral realm where Heaven is located and then being sent to the earth planet. Death then became part of human experience.

In Akan tradition, preserving the purity and sanctity of the soul or *okra* is essential in order for humans to fulfill their destinies and to return to their Great Ancestors, *Nananom Asamanpong*, and finally to be united with God, *Odomankoma*. When a person defiles his soul, *okra*, his *sunsum*, the element that accounts for the character of the person, is weakened and, as a result, the *okra* becomes a fugitive. It tries to find a hiding place from its enemies, and the person eventually loses his *sunsum*. Thus he cannot fulfill his destiny, *nkrabea* or *hyebea*. When the *okra* finally leaves the body, it returns to God to give an account of its earthly existence. After that the *okra* may be allowed to remain in heaven or told to return to the world again.

The Prophet explained rather that when a human dies, the flesh rots and the *okra*, Soul, goes to the astral realm where it had come from. Prophet Amoaforo believed that at death the deceased would go to the first heaven to await trial and judgment, based on his fidelity to the agreement, or *hyebea*, that the Creator delivered before birth. Those who have not fulfilled their destinies while on earth are sent back to this planet. They might have to return to earth in a series of reincarnations until they are worthy to reach the ultimate heaven and be reunited with God. Prophet Amoaforo said, "Development takes a long time. As one reincarnates, he develops."

Prophet Amoaforo further stated, "If I pass away, my Head Prophet Ankomah can help me by sending me to heaven. This he can do, but if I am myself not spiritually perfectly developed, then I would have to come back to the earth and do a lot more learning towards spiritual perfection. I have to learn and pass the basic requirement.

True, anyone can get to heaven, as Jesus said to the sinner, 'Today you will be with me in paradise.' One can get to heaven, but if the person is not spiritually and perfectly developed, he or she would have to return to the earth and repeat the learning process again. Christians generally think that once people die they go to heaven. In the Prophet's thought, they will return to the earth if they did not pass the fundamental requirements. This is what is referred to as the process of reincarnation, which most Christians reject. The process can be compared to academic studies at the universities, where, as you know, there are several levels of degrees."

Christian theology on judgment and the afterlife evolved historically, but, as Prophet Amoaforo has stated, in orthodox forms of Christian theology, reincarnation has not been accepted as a way of making recompense for sin. Rather, a system for judging souls on the way in which they lived their human lives evolved in early Christianity. The result of this hierarchy of sin means that the soul might be condemned to hell for eternal punishment, sent to an intermediate place of purification called purgatory or rewarded for a good life by being enabled to enter heaven for the rest of eternity.

Jesus, according to Prophet Amoaforo, originally came from the 25th planet, a planet of shepherds. This signified that he was to tend the sheep, human beings, thus his self-designation as the Good Shepherd. The Prophet explained, "Shepherds have patience for their flock. Likewise, a leader of people should have love and patience for them. The star that led the wise men to Jesus was *Ratani*, a star from the 25th planet as well. *Ratani* also appeared to inform the shepherds that Christ from their planet had arrived on earth." Prophet Amoaforo has said that he was once taken to the 25th planet, the planet of shepherds. He reported that the staff shepherds hold is a staff of love. Further, Jesus was born in a manger not because there was no other place in Bethlehem for him to be born but because Jesus wanted it to be known that he came from the 25th planet.

According to Prophet Amoaforo, Jesus was not a divinity. His personal mission was to set an example for the way that humans should live in order to reach their final destiny. When his life here ended, Jesus, who had come from the 25th planet, returned to the 75th planet, because he had finished his assignment well on earth.

He will not be here again but he can help us in the astral world. This view that Jesus was not divine does not, generally, fall within the scope of orthodox Christian belief.

Prophet Amoaforo claimed that he was or was about to become an "ascended master" at the time of his death in 2006. He also reported that he had previously reincarnated in the past as a shepherd, then as a fisherman and owned several fishing boats, and also as a farmer. The Prophet regularly reported seeing souls in the astral realm and knew at which planetary levels they had arrived in their personal journeys. He was also able to complete journeys to other places on earth, such as India, Australia, and Italy.

The spirit can wield influence or control over human beings. Thus, the interaction between spirit and matter, and between spiritual beings and human beings, is understood as falling within the range of human experience. It is in relationship to the divinity that the need for intermediaries arises. The ancestors and spirits perform this role for humans in African thought. The world of spirits and ancestors and the world of humans interpenetrate each other, and communication can be initiated by spiritual agents, such as the angels, and also by human agents like Prophet Amoaforo.

While it repudiated many other aspects of traditional culture, Christianity does have a category of intermediate spirit beings between God and humans. Instead of being named in relation to their functions in the natural world, such entities in Christian cosmology are called angels or demons, depending on their dispositions. At times in the Hebrew and Christian Scriptures and traditions, they are given specific names, such as *Michael* and *Lucifer*. Prophet Amoaforo knew angels by these names, but he also mentioned many angels with names that are neither traditional nor Christian.

Prophet Amoaforo worked among people who believed in a world populated with angels and demons. There are, as we have seen, many stories of the Prophet confronting people who worked with evil spirits, and defeating the demons. He often converted those defeated practitioners to Musama Christianity, as well. These accounts illustrate that he and they accepted a dualistic worldview as a reality in their lives. As we have already seen, Prophet Amoaforo fully adopted the eschatology of the Christian missionaries and the prophets of the Musama Disco Christo Church, who taught that the end of the world was made manifest in natural events. All three traditions also hold that the preservation of the purity of the soul is the ultimate requirement that humans must meet in order to fulfill their personal destiny: to join the ancestors, and ultimately to be reunited with God.

Mehu, like the Musama church and other forms of Christianity, also considers itself an inclusive community open to people of all ethnicities, races, and religions. Prophet Amoaforo has stated, "Our mission here accepts all groups, sects, and religious faiths. We even accept Moslems who come here often and always make great donations to us. The Moslems come here for worship. The point is that anything that is done for the glory of God is good. In fact, all religious sects are good. The critical thing is the leadership that is directed by the right spirit."

Prophet Amoaforo asserted that Mehu is intended not for Africans alone but for the peoples of the whole world. This belief is illustrated graphically at Mehu in one wall painting's juxtaposition of a portrait of the first head of the Musama Disco Christo Church, Jemisimiham Jehu-Appiah, who represents black people; a painting of crossed British and French flags, representing white people; and Jesus, through whom blacks and whites are united.

On a large wall near the entrance to Mehu and constructed late in Prophet Amoaforo's life is a representation of *Huhuuma*, the key of the planets, and a list of those who are welcome at Mehu: "All powers belong to Jehovah, All Christian churches, Spiritual churches, Islam, Freemason, Odd Fellow, Hindu, Buddhism, Hare Krishna, Yoga, Eckankar, Fetishism, Bahai, Judaism." Prophet Amoaforo's inclusivity was also revealed in portraits of Gandhi, Sri Probhupada, Mohammed, Krishna and his Mother, Yasoda, at Mehu.

Prophet Amoaforo regarded the mission of the Musama Disco Christo Church to be, first, preaching the true gospel of the unity of all religions, races, and nations with a common destiny and, second, healing diseases of all kinds and protecting and delivering people from the destructive forces of the devil and other demonic spirits, whether in heaven, on earth, under the earth, or in the sea.

When asked what role he had in the Musama Disco Christo

Theology

Church, Prophet Amoaforo said that, in addition to healing and feeding the people who came to Mehu with the produce of his fish farms and crop farms, namely, being a saviour to people, his role was to unite all religions and all races of all nations and bring them together to realize the universal brotherhood of mankind. This vision of the universal brotherhood of mankind prompted Prophet Amoaforo to travel astrally around the world on his preaching and healing missions and to welcome people of all persuasions to Mehu. Most missionary churches in Ghana, however, expected faithful adherence solely to their forms and expressions of Christianity.

Prophet Amoaforo's official title in the Musama Disco Christo Church was Prophet, indicating his functional status as a healer and a prophetic figure. In these roles, he certainly excelled, thanks to the special spiritual gifts he had been given. These are the abilities for which he has been most noteworthy, thanks in large part to his accomplishments at Mehu.

Prophet Amoaforo's capacity to travel to the astral realm is beyond the current developmental stage of most human beings, but it is an ability that he tried to train people to achieve, since all people have these latent natural capacities and special spiritual gifts.

Prophet Amoaforo's astuteness and creativity as a theologian is perhaps one of his greatest gifts, an intellectual gift in the last analysis, although it is remarked upon least among his accomplishments. The systematization he undertook of Akan beliefs, biblical teachings, Musama beliefs and practices and his own spiritual experiences, achieved over years of reflection and practice, can be viewed as a remarkable expression of African religiosity.

The integration the Prophet achieved of Akan beliefs with his own spiritual experiences and Christian cosmological and theological views demanded a creative new conceptualization of all of these elements. He related both his prophetic and healing missions with his cosmology and angelology. And his adoption of the Musama teaching on the inclusivity of all religions transcended the narrower exclusivity of the biblical traditions, both Jewish and Christian, as well as the colonial interpretation of Christianity.

Prophet Amoaforo identified himself as an "ascended master," one of a select spiritual group who met periodically in the astral realm to run the world. Others might consider him an avatar, as he considered Jesus to be.

Prophet Amoaforo may not himself have realized the extent of his extraordinary accomplishments. The proverb that says no one is capable of putting his/her arms completely around the baobab tree of truth, but Prophet Amoaforo certainly came very close to accomplishing that in his world and for his time.

Afterword

Jenasman Kwadwo Amoaforo, Senior Superintendent Prophet of the Musama Disco Christo Church, was a twentieth century Ghanaian holy man who lived his life in accordance with what he sincerely believed was God's plan for him. His encounter with the founder of the Musama Disco Christo Church, the Prophet Jemisimiham Jehu-Appiah, who ordained him as a Junior Prophet in 1943, began his lifelong journey as a Prophet – delivering prophecies, healing people with various ailments, giving needed comfort to the distresssingly weary and painfully afflicted, growing food and rearing fish to feed the hungry, and uniting people of all religions and races of all nations and bringing them together to realize the Universal Brotherhood of Humankind.

Like the prophets in biblical times, Jenasman Kwadwo Amoaforo conscientiously stood up to the powers-that-be in the Musama Disco Christo Church. He raised his voice against perfidious wrongdoings in high places in the church and foretold the consequences of these misdeeds, resulting in the removal of the head of the church, Prophet Miritaiah Jonah Jehu-Appiah, Akaboha III. And, for daring to speak so boldly and openly in 1979, he was severely castigated and suspended, virtually being made a pariah. But he was vindicated as events began to unfold during the church crisis in 2003, and a new head of the church was appointed, in the person of the Akaboha IV, Prophet Moknajeeba Fiifi Jehu-Appiah. But in all this, Jenasman Kwadwo Amoaforo humbly regarded himself not so much the predictor of momentous events, but rather the instrument of what needed to be said in order to set things right.

As a magnanimously compassionate person, Jenasman Kwadwo Amoaforo was never uncivil towards anyone. It was unimaginable that he would have behaved disrespectfully, even toward those who would try to revile or slander him, for to behave otherwise would have amounted to going against his own consciousness of humaneness and humility. Besides, he was guided in his conduct by a favourite saying of his, that we must do to others as we would have them do to us, because everything we do will come back, either to bless us or torment us.

He dedicated his life, a life of deep spirituality and faith, to serving countless others and meeting their needs. And in this way, he achieved greatness, for as Martin Luther King, Jr. said, "Everyone has the power for greatness, not fame, but greatness, because greatness is determined by service". Looking over the entire spectrum of his life and taking account of the myriad services he rendered, it becomes clear that he entered this world with a temperament, personality, and spirit that was earnestly passionate about humanity, and he spent his whole life serving others. It is this observation that was captured in one of the eulogies at his funeral in 2006, "Perhaps without knowing, and certainly without saying, Prophet Amoaforo acted as God's child and God's agent, even perhaps as one of God's angels."

Above all, he was open and tolerant towards other religious persuasions and never uttered a condemnatory word about religions that differed from his own, but instead sought to interact with their adherents. His religious orientation was firmly grounded in his Akan culture that espouses openness, and this influenced his practice of Christianity. And in an age characterized by increasing religious intolerance, Prophet Jenasman Kwadwo Amoaforo's stance was refreshingly commendable. His memory will stand as a gleaming beacon to all those who search for religious peace in our world.